Clinical Encounters and the Lacanian Analyst

Clinical Encounters and the Lacanian Analyst presents interviews with Lacanian analysts, exploring their professional development and the effects that their patients have had on them.

Dries Dulsster interviews leading Lacanian psychoanalysts, asking them for insights on the formative effects of working with their analysands. By asking *"Who's your Dora?"*, Dulsster invites the interviewees to reflect on the patients who have changed their practice or influenced the development of key theories.

Clinical Encounters and the Lacanian Analyst will be of great interest to practicing and training Lacanian analysts, as well as to Lacanian scholars and academics.

Dries G. M. Dulsster is Internship Coordinator and Educational Supervisor at the Department of Psychoanalysis and Clinical Consulting, Ghent University, Belgium. He works as a psychoanalyst in a private practice and is Editor in Chief of the *Psychoanalytische Perspectieven*.

"In his postscript to *The Question of Lay Analysis*, Freud famously stated that a psychoanalyst cannot treat a patient without learning something new. And indeed, it would not be an exaggeration to say that it was the young woman Freud called 'Dora' who taught him about the importance of transference. In this riveting set of frank interviews with an international cast of practicing psychoanalysts, which is bookended by two contextualising reflections, Dulsster uses this 'Dora-principle' to ask his interlocutors about the patients who helped shape their own clinical work. The result is a truly original and invariably fascinating series of reflections on how all psychoanalysts come to reinvent clinical practice for themselves by virtue of their patients. This book is essential reading for trainees and established clinicians alike, across the spectrum of mental health care providers."

Dany Nobus, Professor of Psychoanalytic Psychology, Brunel University London, UK; Founding Scholar, British Psychoanalytic Council

"At last(!), a compelling 'spoken' account of Lacanian clinical work which relies on the verbal interchange rather than on theoretical exposition in order to re-orient us regards fundamental psychoanalytic concepts. In an inspired move, Dulsster invites many of the most renowned Lacanian practitioners onto the couch so as to reflect on their formative experiences as clinicians. What emerges is an essential account of the idiosyncrasies underlying psychoanalytic formation and of the singularity of what it means to truly listen to those who enter the analytic situation."

Derek Hook, Associate Professor of Psychology, Duquesne University, USA; co-editor of the Reading Lacan's Ecrits series; and author of *Six Moments in Lacan* (both Routledge)

"*Clinical Encounters and the Lacanian Analyst* is an inspiring text for both new and seasoned psychoanalysts. With an exquisite light touch, Dulsster interviews nine practitioners who generously offer their clinical resourcefulness and dexterity, as well as share fertile moments of speech effects for both the patient and the analyst, including those of failure, in cases that are significant to their own formation. The book shows how patients teach analysts to be better analysts. It demystifies Lacanian practice, highlights its diversity, and demonstrates its power and relevance in any healthcare setting. Once you pick up this book, you won't be able to put it down. It's a great read!"

Eve Watson, psychoanalyst, Dublin, Ireland; co-editor of *Critical Essays on the Drive: Lacanian Theory and Practice* (Routledge)

Clinical Encounters and the Lacanian Analyst

"Who's your Dora?"

Dries G. M. Dulsster

Routledge
Taylor & Francis Group

LONDON AND NEW YORK

Designed cover image: Saul Leiter, 'Joanna', 1947.

First published 2024
by Routledge
4 Park Square, Milton Park, Abingdon, Oxon OX14 4RN

and by Routledge
605 Third Avenue, New York, NY 10158

Routledge is an imprint of the Taylor & Francis Group, an informa business

British Library Cataloguing-in-Publication Data
A catalogue record for this book is available from the British Library

Library of Congress Cataloging-in-Publication Data
Names: Dulsster, Dries G. M., author.
Title: Clinical encounters and the Lacanian analyst : "who's your Dora?" /
[edited by] Dries G.M. Dulsster.
Description: Abingdon, Oxon ; New York, NY : Routledge, 2024. | Includes
bibliographical references and index. |
Identifiers: LCCN 2023018281 (print) | LCCN 2023018282 (ebook) |
ISBN 9781032532219 (hardback) | ISBN 9781032532202 (paperback) |
ISBN 9781003410935 (ebook)
Subjects: LCSH: Psychotherapist and patient. | Psychoanalysis. | Psychoanalysts--
Interviews. | Lacan, Jacques, 1901-1981.
Classification: LCC RC480.8 .D85 2024 (print) | LCC RC480.8 (ebook) |
DDC 616.89/17--dc23/eng/20230623
LC record available at https://lccn.loc.gov/2023018281
LC ebook record available at https://lccn.loc.gov/2023018282

ISBN: 978-1-032-53221-9 (hbk)
ISBN: 978-1-032-53220-2 (pbk)
ISBN: 978-1-003-41093-5 (ebk)

DOI: 10.4324/9781003410935

Typeset in Times New Roman
by Taylor & Francis Books

Contents

Acknowledgements

This book would not have been possible without psychoanalysts accepting my invitation. I'm forever grateful to Paul Verhaeghe, Stijn Vanheule, Evi Verbeke, Amar El-Omari, Annie Rogers, Stephanie Swales, Kristen Hennessy, Patricia Gherovici and Jamieson Webster. Accepting an invitation to talk about clinical work and the subjective effects these encounters entail is a risk they did not shy away from. For that, they all have my greatest respect.

Additionally, I would also like to thank those who read some of the (first) interviews, giving feedback and responding heartily to the project. Thanks to Emma Acke, Liesbeth Taels, Sarah De Wever and Iris Defrancq. Thanks to Junior Ingouf and Fauve Peirelinck for reading the final draft of the manuscript. Thanks to Yasmin Van 'tveld and Trevor Perri for the copy editing.

I would like to acknowledge Ghent University and the Department of Psychoanalysis and Clinical Consulting. As Educational Supervisor and Internship Coordinator I'm offered a chance to talk and discuss psychoanalytic practice with students, taking their first steps in clinical practice. Their questions and struggles (as my own) inspire me to continue to work on clinical formation.

I would also like to thank all my analysands for the trust they put in me and the formative effects they have and have had on my clinical practice.

Last, I would like to thank Lize, the case I consider to be my Dora. It's an encounter that has resonated throughout all my writings and clinical work.

Chapter 1

Introduction
"Who's your Dora?"

Contingent Encounters

A couple years ago, while presenting a paper on working with psychosis, I clearly remember saying to the audience: "This is the last time I'm going to discuss this case."

This has been a lie.

When I present papers on psychosis, working with trauma, and dealing with suicidal ideation; when I discuss the matter of diagnostics or try to explain the object *a*, my encounter with Lize immediately comes to mind. There seems to be no escape. Working with Lize has illustrated so much of psychoanalytic theory for me, all the while making clear that I don't even need theory to work with patients. You have to listen to them and see where the process brings you.

Throughout the years, talking with friends about their clinical experiences, listening to psychoanalysts at conferences or colleagues teaching at the university, it seemed that a lot of them (if not all) seem to have the same experience. They all had contingent encounters that formed them as clinicians, had a propelling effect in their own analysis, helped them elaborate on psychoanalytic theory and so on.

Although this is striking, it should come as no surprise. Freud's findings and theoretical elaborations were the result of contingent encounters with his patients. A good example is that of Emmy von N., where one could argue that the idea of free association does not originate from Freud but from Emmy. In his *Studies on Hysteria* (Freud, 1955 [1983], p. 63), discussing his work with Emmy, Freud states:

> I took an opportunity of asking her, too, why she had gastric pains and what they came from (…) She then said in a definitely grumbling tone that I was not to keep on asking her where this and that came from, but to let her tell me what she had to say. I fell in with this, and she went on without preface….

DOI: 10.4324/9781003410935-1

The development of psychoanalysis has only been possible because patients have been tutors for their analysts and psychoanalysts, who have welcomed this.

The case of Anna O., for Breuer and Freud, and the case of Dora for Freud, are other clear examples of this. Through working with Anna, Breuer and Freud were able to create a new, original method for working with mental distress: listening not only to establish a diagnosis but also to effectuate a treatment (Launer, 2005). However, Breuer also stumbled on the deadlock of transference and countertransference: Anna experiencing a phantom pregnancy, delivering Breuer's imaginary baby; Breuer himself having strong feelings of affection for Anna. As an effect, Breuer decided to terminate the treatment and transferred her to Freud. Where for Breuer, working with Anna was an ending – never again! – for Freud it was a beginning (Geerardyn, 1993). Breuer backed down and did not want to know – Freud on the other hand wanted to know and continued his research on 'the talking cure'.

Freud's Dora

Now, although Freud wanted to know – he kept imposing his own theories on his patients. Indeed, for a long time Freud positioned himself as the master of the unconscious, doing his patients little good (Fink, 2017). The Dora-case (Freud, 1953 [1905]) illustrates Freud trying to figure everything out himself as quickly as possible, wanting to be right. Freud interpreted Dora's symptoms and behaviour in a way that fitted his own theories, rather than objectively observing them. He imposed his own views and desires onto Dora and ignored her own perspective. The Dora case is known as a 'Fragment of an Analysis of a Case of Hysteria', a fragment, because Dora ended the treatment and did not return to see Freud. She gave him his two-week notice. Freud had missed the homosexual interest of Dora in another woman, neglecting the question of femineity that was at stake, this because of his own beliefs on the matter.

Freud was shaken awake by Dora and as stated by Fink (2017, p. 190), "Freud was obviously very hurt when Dora quit therapy and it could be argued that writing the famous case study was a way to figure out what went wrong and to find a way to get over her." Some of the greatest work in music or literature originate from such (tragic) encounters.

Considering all this, Freud makes it clear that his patients were his tutors, provoking further theoretical elaborations and clinical know-how. It is obvious Freud learned from his mistakes, and he became a psychoanalyst by starting to listen to his hysteric patients and by acknowledging that he was involved in, and influenced by, the process of what his patients were saying (Miller, 1993). Lacan, on the other hand, started by listening to a psychotic patient, namely Aimée (Lacan, 2015 [1932]) and elaborated his thesis on her case. Lacan studied her paranoid psychosis and delirious writings. Miller (1993) states that it was this encounter that led Lacan to psychoanalysis and as such impacted his clinical formation.

Freud and Lacan are not the only ones. Anne Lysy (2002), a former Analyst of the School, discussed her formation as an analyst and recounted a clinical case presentation that had a profound effect on her. She was struck by the rigorousness and precision of the young psychotic woman, which dazzled her. Lysy also stated that sometimes an answer from one of her analysands brutally questions her position in analytic work. Similarly, Alexandre Stevens (2002), founder of *Le Courtil* and former president of the New Lacanian School, talks about the psychotic patients he encountered in the institution and how they helped him orient himself in analytic work. These examples demonstrate the crucial role that analysands play in the training of each analyst. We would argue that each case puts the psychoanalyst and psychoanalysis to the test, challenging the knowledge of the psychoanalyst and the theory of psychoanalysis.

As I already stated, the same was true for me.

My Own Dora

During one of the first weeks of my internship, Lize comes up to me and wants to talk to me personally (Dulsster, 2015). I accept and Lize tells me she's been dating a fellow patient for a while now. This makes it impossible for her to speak in the group therapy. She can't tell the staff about this because they would ask her to leave the institution. She doesn't really consider me to be a staff member, so she feels she can tell me this in trust. From that point on, Lize came to talk to me for about a half-an-hour a week, keeping her mouth shut in group therapy.

Lize told me she was admitted when her parents had found her farewell letters. She could no longer bear what had happened to her. A few years before, one of the neighbour kids had taken advantage of her. While playing on the street, he asked her to come join him in his room. She saw no harm in it, but once they were in his room, he started touching her. A few weeks later, the same thing happened. She doesn't understand why she went along with it a second time: "as if once wasn't bad enough". She hadn't talked about this to anyone, but recently it became more and more difficult to bear. She stressed that she doesn't want to talk about it, it would be too much.

The fact that she was permitted to have individual conversations with me was short lived. The team insisted it was important that she also talked to them, and, more specifically, talk about her trauma. One of the main ideas in the institution was that speaking helps. She was told speaking was important, that it would relieve the trauma, release the tension, that she could 'discharge'. Lize constantly indicated that she was afraid to open Pandora's box, but after long insistence of the entire team (and me as well), she finally started to talk about her traumatic experiences.

The staff were very happy they had finally been able to break her resistance. However, some other things started to happen... She started to seriously cut herself. Where she previously had just been superficially scratching her arms, she now had to be taken to the emergency room for stitches. She said she wanted to cut herself to shreds: "My body is broken; the others can do with it whatever they want." The staff weren't panicking: "Lize has to go through the trauma, continue to symbolize it." They proposed a more intensive therapy: she had to speak more and more and was placed under increased supervision. Every half-an-hour a nurse came to look at her. From then on, she had to go to the emergency room daily. Even in therapy, Lize seemed to slip away. She came apart at the seams. In group therapy, she cringed into a small ball. In the creative therapies, she presented only despair: black paintings, with just a small dot of red in the middle. During her free time, she made patchworks with characters being destroyed, beaten to pulp, bloody faces all over. There was nothing left but blood and despair. Talking about her traumatic experiences seemed to have dramatic effects. She started cutting her thighs and pubic area daily. She was reliving the abuse even more, images of the abuse imposing themselves on her.

When one of the nurses noted that talking about the traumatic events doesn't seem to do her much good, Lize herself says: "I have to go through it, what else am I doing here? You all asked me to talk, didn't you?" However, the same remark kept reappearing at the staff meetings: "she has to go through it, we must not shy away from the difficult work". Nevertheless, Lize tried to make something clear to us: "I'd rather go through physical hell than through the hell of words. If I don't talk about it, then it's not true, then it didn't happen."

Lize indicated that her words were powerless against the real of the trauma and it is safe to say talking that way didn't help her. The words were cutting her. Her speaking didn't process the trauma, but made it happen again and again.

Seeing the effect the therapy had really shook me up. It made me discuss the case with a supervisor at the university. There, I got the suggestion that, because of language having effects in the real, instead of the level of the symbolic, Lize probably had a psychotic structure. This wasn't something they were considering at the psychiatric ward. There, Lize had gotten the following diagnosis: 'Dysthymic disorder, mixed neurotic and abandonment type, post-traumatic stress disorder. Avoidant attachments behind which lie unresolved dependency needs. Borderline personality traits. Shortage of felt safety.' For me, this was a first confrontation with the function of diagnostics and the associated therapy. This DSM-diagnosis seemed to be a mere indication of clinical phenomena and does not question the function of specific symptoms. Although already having theoretically learned that the DSM was an a-theoretical model which reduced the diagnostic process to merely a process of nomination, it was an encounter with the fact that these diagnoses said nothing about a possible orientation for the treatment. Using a diagnosis should be an act which implies a decision with clear indications for the direction of the treatment. This is what is at stake in diagnostics from a Lacanian perspective: we look at the logic and function of the symptoms, and this makes us orient our treatment accordingly. From a Lacanian point of view, there's an essential difference between the analysis of what is repressed, such as working with neurosis, as the tempering of an inundating drive working with psychosis. Lize made clear to me that there was a jouissance in language. Words are not just dead symbols; they are equally infused with jouissance. She indicated how some speaking beings don't inhabit language but are inhabited by it. They are cut by it. Lize taught me we should never force patients to speak about the past or any traumatic events. It's free associations, so that does not mean: 'freely associate on this topic'. Listening to Lize, we had to stop making her speak about her trauma and stop identifying her as a trauma patient.

During one of our sessions, Lize brought some personal notes in which she had charted her cutting behaviour. She wrote down what she felt before she cut, after she cut and why she cut. She did this because she thought she was expected to do so. It came to mind that she blamed the staff for reducing everything to her traumatic experience, and instead of going along with this, I asked her to put those things aside and just asked her how she was feeling that day and what she was going to do for the rest of the day. In the following sessions, we started talking about her hobbies, steering the conversation away from the traumatic story. I tried to make clear that everybody has problems with sexuality, that love is troublesome for everyone, that this is not necessarily always related to the trauma she had experienced. Slowly, a different perspective on the traumatic experience started to emerge. She felt angry because she had to go to therapy. She felt angry that she must pay for what he did to her: "He has taken away all possibilities to build a normal life!" She also started to question: "Why am I cutting in the pubic area? Nothing ever happened there." As such, she started to discuss problems regarding femininity: "I couldn't allow my mother to see that I was a girl." She wanted to keep her femininity hidden from her mother's gaze. Something she experienced as being very traumatic was the fact that when she was little and was playing in her bedroom, her mother would open the door to see what she was doing and just stare at her. It perplexed her. She had the same experience with her fellow patient with whom she has a relationship: "I cannot bear his eager look." The 'eager look' also puts the intervention of the staff to 'check up on her every half hour' in a whole new perspective: the trauma of the gaze was repeated every half hour. For Lize, the gaze was not mediated by desire, but a raw traumatic experience of the real.

Now, listening to what she said, one can hear guidelines for a direction of the treatment. First and foremost, we had to castrate our gazes. Everything she said about the gaze showed that there was a singular logic at stake, and this had to be taken into account. In addition, talking about the experience with her neighbour wasn't helping her at all, and we had to invent a different way of speaking. Consequently, instead of the regular face-to-face sessions, we went out for a walk, and, as already indicated, we started talking about what interested her, like how she could enjoy listening to Pergolesi's 'Stabat Mater', which she used to listen to together with her grandfather. We also talked about everyday topics, such as art, literature, nature and love. These conversations helped her to find ways to fix the overwhelming jouissance. With her therapist, she started to discuss the difficulties of building a normal life, how she experienced contact with others and the way she thought about herself. This way of working, following Lize's logic instead of that of the team, made life more bearable for her and offered a way out.

Other Dora's

It was clear that the Lacanian viewpoint on diagnostics, Lacanian theory concerning language, jouissance and the gaze, and the accompanying treatment helped me thinking about the case of Lize. It made me want to fully dedicate myself to Lacanian psychoanalysis but also made me consult an analyst, discussing, among other things, what I experienced during this internship.

Given the impact of my encounter with Lize and listening to others discuss cases, I became curious about the effects of clinical work on psychoanalytic scholars and clinicians. Specifically, I wanted to know how clinical work affects both their psychoanalytic practice and their theoretical work. So, I decided to ask them directly. Which patients come to mind and what can we learn from this? Therefore, I contacted psychoanalysts to talk about their clinical practice and almost all of them responded enthusiastically.

For everyone the interview started with the same question: "Who is your Dora?"

References

Dulsster, D. (2015). Woorden die Snijden [When Words Cut]. *Tijdschrift voor Psycho-analyse*, 2, 98–106.

Fink, B. (2017). *A Clinical Introduction to Freud*. W.W. Norton & Company, Inc., New York.

Freud, S. (1953 [1901]). *Fragments of an Analysis of a Case of Hysteria. Standard Edition*, VII, The Hogarth Press, London, 1–122.

Freud, S. (1955 [1893]). *Studies on Hysteria*. The Hogarth Press Limited, London.

Geerardyn, F. (1993). *Freuds Psychologie van het Oordeel [Freud's Psychology of the Judgment]*. Idesça, Ghent.

Lacan, J. (2015 [1932]). *De la Psychose Paranoïaque dans ses Rapports avec la Personnalité*. Points.

Launer, J. (2005). Anna O and the 'Talking Cure'. *QJM: An International Journal of Medicine*, 98 (6), 465–466. Downloaded on 3rd of June from: https://doi.org/10.1093/qjmed/hci068.

Lysy, A. (2002). Témoignages sur la formation [Testimonies on Clinical Formation]. *Quarto*, 76, 31–36.

Miller, J.-A. (1993). Lesson de 8 Décembre 1993. *L'Orientation Lacanienne: Donc* (unpublished).

Stevens, A. (2002). Témoignages sur la formation. Clinique de la formation dans la psychanalyse. *Quarto*, 76, 48–49.

Chapter 2

Paul Verhaeghe – Remarks That Resonate

Paul Verhaeghe is Emeritus Professor at Ghent University and a Lacanian psychoanalyst. He obtained a PhD in clinical psychology and a special doctorate in psychodiagnostics. He received the Goethe Award for the US edition of his book *On Being Normal and Other Disorders* (2008), in which he offers an alternative to the DSM diagnostic system. He is the author of books such as *Does the Woman Exist? From Freud's Hysteric to Lacan's Feminine* (1999) and *Love in a Time of Loneliness* (2011). Throughout his career his attention has increasingly focused on the combined effects of changes in society and work organisation. The publication of his lecture at the Oikos Academy was awarded 'essay of the year' in 2011 by Liberales.

Dries Dulsster (DD): I would first like to thank you for taking part in this project concerning the question: "Who is your Dora?" This is the first interview of the series, so I don't have a clear idea yet of where it will lead us. The reason why I decided to start off with you, is because you are the one who introduced me to psychoanalysis. It's not unimportant to note that you did that with a case through which you pointed out some problematic aspects of clinical diagnostics. It concerned a young man who stole Mercedes cars and then took them on a joyride.

Paul Verhaeghe (PV): That is a case from a very long time ago, from shortly after I graduated. I have to say I had a very different clinical practice then compared to now.

DD: How so?

PV: At the time I was working in a centre for special youth care. After graduating, I had a substitute contract in a centre for mental health care in Sint-Niklaas, where I got acquainted with fairly classical psychotherapy with middle-class clients. After my civilian service, I started working in special youth care, which was a completely different practice. I was constantly confronted with the importance of people's social backgrounds, and I learned a lot about diagnostics. When I was offered the position of PhD student, I was

DOI: 10.4324/9781003410935-2

in doubt for a long time whether I wanted to go back to university. At the treatment centre, I was head of the youngest group. There was no psychiatrist to oversee our work, so we were quite free. It wasn't like it is today. The group I was working with consisted of sixteen to eighteen young boys between the ages of 12 and 16. They stayed with us for a minimum of three months for observation and treatment. We made diagnostic reports and based on those reports the juvenile court decided on these young people's further course. There were two of us, and my colleague approached everything from the viewpoint of test diagnostics, but that was not my cup of tea. Twice a week, I had the time to see these young people in my office individually. However, I realised very quickly that some of them were still children, and that I had a better chance of getting to know them by going outside and playing football. Consider it a form of broader play therapy. I learned a lot during my time there. It is where my interest in social backgrounds stems from, since many of those young people came from rather marginalised communities. The boy you refer to, however, did not. He was 16 and already an adolescent. You could talk to him, and that was actually a form of conversational therapy. He had been caught by the police while joyriding and, as it was not the first time, the juvenile court threatened to take action. We were not only expected to formulate a diagnosis, but also to provide rapid treatment. I noticed very quickly that he did not steal just any car; it had to be a Mercedes every time. He drove it around almost aimlessly, always alone, only to leave it undamaged in one particular province of the country, after which he hitchhiked back home. He could not explain his behaviour. Now, instead of test-diagnostics, I talked with him, and I listened to him. It turned out that he was an only child, and that his parents were in the middle of a marriage crisis. His father came from a lower-class family, but had been able to climb the socio-economic ladder. His mother came from a middle-class family. It came to light that the mother had a lover, and that the father was working his ass off in... a Mercedes company. It also turned out that the region where the boy left the cars was his mother's native region. That's why earlier I said: "almost aimless". As I have written in my book, it appears that the son was split between his father and his mother. Psychoanalytically, his behaviour could be interpreted as a response to the desires of both his father and his mother. It was very fascinating for me to see what happened there, beyond the all-too-easy explanation of 'joyriding'. The question nobody had asked before was why every time it had to be a Mercedes. It is by talking and listening to someone that you get answers – much faster than you'd expect. And then you start seeing how the family's story is intertwined with his behaviour, and as a rookie you suddenly start to understand psychoanalysis... Freud, Lacan... they're right! They're just right!

DD: This anecdote had an impact on me when I was a student. It illustrated that, concerning symptoms, something else was at stake. It was something he illustrated to you, being a rookie, as well.

PV: It was my introduction to clinical diagnostics in a clinical practice. Those young people were with us twenty-four seven. We participated in the community groups, I had dinner with these children, I sat at the table with them... Yet, I have always been careful to not become one of them, and to remain outside and above – which was much easier in those days, because there was more authority. I worked with a very good social worker who did thorough social research. I got a picture of their social backgrounds thanks to her. We also saw their parents, if they showed up, and there was a medical examination done. The latter did not amount to much, because the children were healthy. ADHD did not yet exist. These circumstances also painted a picture of how they behaved towards their peers, towards educators, towards you. You never get that in a normal outpatient practice. We were able to write a well-rounded diagnostic report – luckily, we didn't use labels at the time. The way we worked was close to anti-psychiatry. I am afraid this is no longer how it works nowadays. You may have noticed that in recent years, I have put an increasing emphasis on social factors. That's still a result from my experiences in that centre.

DD: Many of your books do indeed put emphasis on social aspects: identity, authority, intimacy... However, the book that, for me, really stands out is *On Being Normal and Other Disorders*.[1] It's a book with a clear clinical purpose, as is indicated with the case of the boy with the Mercedes.

PV: My experience in special youth care was an eye-opener, and played a part in the writing of this book. You also have to see this book on diagnostics in the context of its time. I was working as a first assistant when there was a staffing reform at the university. I was appointed associate professor together with six older colleagues, but some of them were angry that I was appointed at such a young age. You may wonder what this has to do with diagnostics, but that period in time was strongly affected by the anti-psychiatry movement, and none of the older professors wanted to burn their fingers on diagnostics, so it was passed on to me, the youngest. I started to apply myself to it. That then became my second doctorate, starting with the three Lacanian subject structures and discourse theory. By then I had also gained more clinical experience, because I had always kept my private practice in the wake of my first practical experiences in a centre for mental health care. So, *On Being Normal and Other Disorders* was strongly influenced by those practical experiences, and that is also why it is so clinical.

DD: I remember from your lectures that the first part of the book was a critical examination of diagnostics. The second part then consists of a background theory that elaborates on an alternative, which is indeed based on discourse theory and the three structures, but, perhaps more importantly, also on something original: the idea of actual pathology.

PV: I have to say that originality does not exist, that's why Lacan says: "There's no symbolic ownership." I got the idea of actual pathology from Freud. That idea was lying there under some dust, forgotten about. I just developed it further, and gradually linked it to identity development and research into the importance of affects. There may be something original in it, but I didn't invent sliced bread.

DD: There are indeed some things there that come together theoretically, but I can't help thinking that it also stems from a clinical clash.

PV: That's for sure.

DD: Given the theme of these interviews, I am very interested in that part.

PV: Of course. How should I put it… If you have a typical psychoanalytic practice in combination with a university degree, chances are you'll only see patients from the bourgeoisie. That is, contemporary forms of psychoneurosis, contemporary variants of hysteria, of obsessional neurosis, or a mixture of these. Classical theory suffices in those cases, and there is no need to change your approach. However, many people I've met in the centre for mental health care have followed me into my private practice. Add my experience in special youth care to the mix, and then you'll understand why I focus on social issues. I have made the very conscious choice to keep seeing people who are socially disadvantaged. I have also always tried to ensure that there is a gender balance in my practice – as many men as women – preferably with as many different issues as possible. Though the issue of psychosis has fallen somewhat outside of this scope. It's not that I didn't have psychotic people in my practice, but they were exceptions. Either way, the fact that I work with issues that fall outside of the classic psychoneurosis means I've seen different things. Let's face it, working with hysterical people is very easy. You push a button, and they start to speak. It is characteristic of hysteria that free association runs automatically. With obsessive-compulsive disorder, it is slightly different, but even then. However, people with anxiety issues, panic disorders, somatization… They sit there and have nothing to say. Nothing comes out. To say that these people are therapy resistant is crazy. But it does mean that as a therapist you have to start looking. I had read all those texts by Freud about the anxiety neurosis, and I recognised it. I saw several unexplained somatic symptoms which I couldn't do much with at first, because between 1985 and 1995, a number of Lacanians interpreted them as a special form of conversion. But I immediately knew that this reasoning was wrong. I know conversion very well. My first PhD was on hysteria, and this was not a conversion. I thought it was too easy to understand it like that. That is not to say that I immediately understood what those somatization phenomena were, that took me some more time, but I did understand panic attacks in a Freudian way. I quite quickly linked up the actual pathology as described by Freud with identity development and affect management, and one thing led to another. I then quickly understood that these people had to be worked with differently. Instead of deconstruction, because an analysis is a deconstruction, you need to help them construct.

DD: Can you tell me more about the clinical encounters that inspired you?

PV: A lot of what I've written about actual pathology comes from clinical encounters. I think of this quite young woman who came to me with a very serious addiction problem. Every few weeks she would wake up in the hospital. At some point she realised that she had to do something about it. She had questions like: "How am I going to go on with my life? How do I continue the relationship with my partner?" She also had a bad job at the time. She came to therapy to review her life – she had a clear request for help. It was a therapy on the cutting edge. I never put her on the couch, and I think she would have been diagnosed with borderline. This was someone who was able to question her personal history, and make the connection with the situation she was in. She was actually a textbook example of parentification. Her father was a heavy drug addict, and her mother was an alcoholic. Her parents divorced, and she continued to systematically take care of her father until he disappeared from the scene due to alcohol. It got so out of hand that youth services had to intervene. One effect of this history was that she sought out partners like her father. Men with addiction problems for whom she cared, and who abused her. After a year-and-a-half of therapy or so, she had changed enough so that she was able to leave an abusive relationship. The most important element in this case is that she was hardly in touch with her own body, which, to me, was an example of what I later elaborated on as actual pathology. Not being in touch with your own experience of affect, and yet being able to sense the other person very well is typical for this clinical image – now called hypermentalisation. The question now was how to get past this using an analysis-inspired approach.

DD: You had to invent a new way of working with her?

PV: Indeed, because it wasn't a classical analysis in the sense of deconstruction. It required a lot of active interventions on my part. By active, I mean that I made much clearer connections and provided much more active constructions. It was also one of the first times that I worked face-to-face so systematically. Before that, I almost always worked via the couch, but the preliminary conversations with this patient showed that that was not going to work.

DD: You were also more active in making connections between the parts of her story?

PV: It was about making connections in two directions: 'her versus her body' and 'her versus the others'. Her use of alcohol was episodic. Periodically, she was drinking a lot. We later discovered that there was also a variant of this: crying every so often for two days. Still later, it turned out that some good sex could help her with that. It turned out that the alcohol, crying, and sex, were different ways to get rid of an accumulation of tensions and affects, without her being aware of it. The connection with others showed itself in the work-place, in the repetition of what she had experienced as an adolescent, and how she was behaving as an adult. Both in her work and in her private life she was at the service of the Other, and she was abused, also financially. She had a very strange employment status whereby someone else was taking her money.

DD: How did her drinking problem evolve?

PV: Remember what Lacan says: the 'cure' comes as a bonus, and that's cer-tainly true in the case of actual phenomena – she stopped drinking com-pletely. It's a case that I often discussed in my lectures, because I didn't understand it very well either. However, she was able to understand it very well herself. She could feel when there was about to be an episode where she would be drinking for 48 hours straight. She told me: "It's either 48 hours of drinking or 48 hours of crying." She had no control over it, but afterwards the effect of unloading, of being deflated, was clear. And then she was able to move on again. She had little defence against this cycle, even though she was a strong woman. She assumed a caretaking role and took on all responsi-bilities from others, but this was a strength that came with a significant vulnerability.

DD: You have always seen her face-to-face?

PV: The purpose of a couch is to make sure that people can say things they would otherwise not say, either because of shame, or fear, or for whatever reason – because of the controlling gaze. In that respect, the couch still works. But with her and patients like her, I realised very quickly – I was able to understand this better afterwards based on diagnostic reasoning, but I didn't know that yet – that they wanted to keep control over the other person. They are too anxious. Being on the couch increases their anxiety, and then nothing works anymore. Why would I use a tool that fuels anxiety in these people? A person can only speak freely when they feel safe, if there's no anxiety about what the other – who they can no longer see when laying on the couch – will do. So, as always, the preliminary sessions are important: you have to know who you're dealing with. With patients like her, to this day, I continue work-ing face-to-face. Of course, this is much less comfortable for the therapist. They keep a very sharp eye on you. They read you, albeit often with a wrong interpretation. They see which emotion is present in you correctly, but the explanation they have for it is not always correct. Of course, they are convinced that their interpretation is accurate – why would you be an exception? For several years, this patient clung very strongly to the analysis. The conversations had a supportive function for her. She was given space to talk during these sessions. She was very verbal, and also read a lot. When she came in, she could easily speak for one hour at a time. I had to teach her to speak more slowly so that she and I could actually listen to what she was saying. For the first time I understood that speaking can be a form of acting out as well, with more or less the same function as drinking or crying: it's about draining tension. Talking was a tap that she could turn on, but she wasn't saying senseless things, though she wasn't telling stories either. It was rather a kind of logorrhea, without being psychotic. After about two years, her talking became calmer, and a reflective function came into play. I say two years, but I can't be sure about the time span without my notes. What was quite striking, however, was that the drinking and crying stopped almost from the moment she came to consult me.

DD: Could we say that the alcohol abuse and crying were now reborn in language? That it had connection to the Other?

PV: As soon as I could – it wasn't possible in the beginning – I intervened and halted her speech, so I could force her to listen to what she had to say. I actively intervened in a lot of different matters. I, for example, said about her romantic relationship: "You're doing the same thing as with your father, you have to stop", and that "it was not a partner relationship, but something else", that she was "being used in a way that was not good for anyone". I think no one would ever say things like this in a classical analysis. I think she knew all of this herself already, but she needed to hear it from someone else. And then she left her partner. Additionally, it became gradually clear that her therapy was also a process of grief. She started to remember things about her father, about what had happened. It was a period of mourning, because she loved her father very much. Her relationship with her mother was different, she felt a lot more responsible for her.

DD: As you mentioned, this was clearly a completely different way of working for you.

PV: Yes. I also worked differently with another analysand whom I had met around the same time. With both women I felt I needed to work in a radically different way, since their issues were not classical neurosis. This second woman arrived straight from the crematorium where the father of her child was cremated after he had committed suicide. She too had an addiction; she too was completely disintegrated. I think she survived mainly because there was a child involved, and she knew that she could not afford to slip away. She persevered for the sake of her child.

DD: Being a mother kept her alive?

PV: She said: "His father committed suicide. I can't do that to that child, for his mother to disappear as well." It was a reason for her to keep on living, and also why she came to see me. I also continued to see her face-to-face. These two women had more or less similar problems, like drugs and social marginality. And both have worked their way out. One of them has a stable romantic relationship now. The other has never been able to develop a long-term intimate relationship, but she is still here.

DD: Could you elaborate a bit on the gaze as a necessary support? It seemed to be important in these cases.

PV: There was a difference in both of them. The second lady I'm talking about now really sought out the gaze. It was clear that she needed my gaze to find approval. The other woman I'm talking about sat in front of me, but she didn't really look at me. She turned away out of shame and guilt. For some reason I was convinced that I should not put her on the couch. With the second woman, it was much clearer for me what was going on. There was a lot of silence, massive grief, depression... This case was also much harder to bear and more difficult as a therapist, because I had to be much more active.

DD: Could you make that a bit more concrete?

PV: To give an example, I also fed the second woman. She was going through a severe anorectic period, and she couldn't eat any more. She was starving herself. It might sound crazy, but I had some yoghurt in the fridge. I stood up and got it, and put it in front of her and told her to eat. My practice then became the only place where she ate anything for weeks. I don't think it gets any more active than that. I didn't spoon-feed her, though. She had to eat by herself.

DD: That seems active indeed.

PV: Yes. The same applied to that other woman, when I told her to leave her romantic relationship.

DD: We could say that it was an intervention on the level of jouissance.

PV: It was always making connections, intervening with an explanation within a supporting transference. The remark on her relationship fell on good ground. She probably just needed to hear it from someone else. It is hard to explain why you can do a certain intervention with one person and not with another. Now, the common denominator of both cases was the level of difficulty. They were both patients with a suicide risk at all times. With one of them, the presence of her child provided some reassurance. However, it was very difficult to bear. I saw her frequently, several times a week, with a confrontational directness. These are the people who sit in front of you, read your body language, and make a comment about you, and you know that what they say is correct. And then you just need to swallow it. It's the kind of analysis where you don't fall asleep, where you stay on your *qui vive*, so to speak. These were not the sessions of which you'd like four in a row. That's just not possible. In case of ordinary neuroses, it is possible to be on autopilot occasionally. But here, because it's face-to-face, and because of the sharpness of these patients, you can't afford going about it like that. The second you switch to autopilot, they shoot you down. However, I have to say that these are the people I like to work with the most.

DD: It does seem like these two patients taught you a lot.

PV: Much of what I have written about actual pathology originates from working with them. I have met many other such patients, but they were the first two with whom I had to conclude that my usual way of working was not possible. I couldn't put them on the couch and just sit back. There may have been hysterical elements present, but it was not hysteria. There were of course also many traumatic elements involved, but not like the usual traumatic neurosis. It certainly had nothing to do with psychosis, although both would most likely have been dubbed as ordinary psychosis if we looked at it from a post-Lacanian perspective. They did not have classic drug problems. I had seen a number of patients where addiction had been the primary issue, but that was not the case with either of them, despite the fact that, if you looked at it psychologically, there was serious substance abuse. It was called borderline at the time, but that is such a rubbish diagnosis. I did have the term at the back of my mind – I mentioned it earlier – but I never used it myself in therapy. I was mainly looking for a way to work with them.

DD: What would you say was most innovative about that way of working? It shows at least something of the creativity through which psychoanalysis can appear. It's about a certain construction, but how do you make sure it's not a suggestive therapy?

PV: I don't think suggestion would have worked with either of them. They were both, in their own way, very compelling: the constraint in the contact, what they said, the appeal that came from it. However, they were asking for articulation. Or rather, they both asked for some kind of value judgement. I explicitly told both of them several times: "What you have experienced is not acceptable. It is fundamentally wrong." I had to say it in a manner that didn't victimise them. It is a kind of legal-ethical statement, and it landed very well in both cases. They had a demand for an Other who would offer a different framework for what they had experienced. They wanted a framework from which they could judge and articulate a number of things themselves, again and again. The theory on neurosis only got me so far. I learned a great deal through working with these two women.

DD: It's not just that they taught you a lot; it had formative effects.

PV: It has been formative in all areas. So, it is difficult to specify what I have learned from them concerning the question "Who's your Dora?" It doesn't work like that. I don't think Dora is about cognitive insights. I think it is much more about how someone deals with the existential questions everyone struggles with. However, in the context of "Who's your Dora?", there is one thing I will never forget, and it does concern something on a cognitive level. As I said earlier, they were the kind of patients who can make remarks that wake you up. This was an analysand of roughly my age – I was a lot younger back then – with a very traumatic past. At a certain point, out of the blue, she threw this in my face: "Are you compensating or are you sublimating?" This resonated with me for years. It made me think strongly about my position. You sit there in the seat of a subject-supposed-to-know, and you are either adored or reviled. Either way, it's a position of luxury, you always stay out of harm's way. She completely shattered that comfort by offering two alternatives on another level, neither of which was pleasant. Compensating... Yes... Well... What am I compensating for? Sublimating? Well, that's not exactly the intention... It is important to note that that was someone who hardly knew anything about psychoanalysis. It was really 'in your face'.

DD: You said it resonated for years?

PV: Understanding what she had said on a cognitive level didn't help. I didn't experience some kind of *aha-erlebnis* that made me understand what she meant. It was something that kept playing in the back of my mind, also during other therapeutic sessions. It concerned the question of what position I occupied in clinical work. It was a question that probed what I, myself, got out of the equation. It was a question of abstinence. Was it ethically possible that I got something out of it? Neither compensating nor sublimating can ever be the intention for the analyst. Every so often, this remark haunts my mind. To compensate or to sublimate... I will never forget it.

DD: It's a remark that had a very formative effect.

PV: Yes... But how to explain it?

DD: In an interview where the impact of the patient on the therapist was also questioned, you mentioned that it is about a certain resonance.

PV: Yes, in recent years I have paid particular attention to affects. I am now also convinced that the repression Freud talked about is not about memories, not about representations, but about affects – the primal repression concerns *eingeklemmte* affects and emotions that can be repressed. There's a distinction between 'emotion' and 'affect'. Affect is not conscious, emotion is the conscious upper layer, but it can be completely faked. The lower layer cannot. There is something that ensures that an affect that is present in me can influence you and vice versa, without us being aware of it or being able to put it into words – that is the attunement, the resonance, with clearly active effects, but we can hardly grasp them. Before you know it, you end up in esotericism, and I don't like that.

DD: In one of the interviews I did for my doctoral dissertation,[2] an analyst said that "something of her unconscious had been formed". This analyst knew me a little, and said that she knew I would find that esoteric, but that she could not help but put it into words like that for herself.

PV: You can actually give some hard scientific grounding to that, if only through endocrinology. Not only bees, but also humans have pheromones, and we apparently notice them. We can smell fear, even consciously, but it is usually subliminal perception. Take a look at the simple idea of catharsis, which we have all experienced. When you watch a play or a movie – especially when doing so with a group of people – you can feel a certain effect flowing physically. It can be sadness. It can be relief. It can be anything... How do you explain that? For me, it is resonance, an attunement between the spectator and what is happening on stage, and among the spectators themselves. You can't explain it cognitively. One of such experiences that has stayed with me, because I can't explain it, concerns pure rhythm. Do you know the Japanese Kodo drummers? They were very popular a while back. They use very small drums, as well as drums with a diameter of a few metres. There is no singing, only rhythm for an hour-and-a-half. I saw them perform in the Queen Elisabeth Hall in Antwerp, and it had an indescribable effect on everyone. Experiences like this have a cathartic effect, but I can't say that I can explain what was going on.

DD: Yes, I think about interviews with dancers about the effect of dance. It is extremely fascinating, but also very difficult for them to put into words.

PV: I'm only a spectator in the example I gave. When you are dancing yourself, you can also *feel* it. I think it is a very different experience. But something comes to be in the interaction between the observer and what is happening on stage. That is attunement. I don't like woolly explanations, I've always hated them, and yet here we are. I'm convinced that something similar can happen clinically in certain gifted moments.

DD: "Are you compensation or sublimating?", Emmy saying: "When are you going to listen to me?" Dora giving Freud his two-week notice. These are the comments that change our clinical practice and theoretical elaborations.

PV: Freud probably received that remark, because he himself wanted to have the floor far too much. Silence is the most important analytical tool – some analysts still don't understand that. The comment of which I was on the receiving end was probably made because it held a grain of truth as well. It touched on a certain unconscious truth.

DD: It may be an intimate question, but would you like to share that truth?

PV: Sure. It's obvious, though you have to take the age I was at the time into account. At that age, people want to be sexually attractive, and as a therapist, I had several female analysands looking at me. You're sitting there in your chair, which is a safe spot, but at the same time... Her remark pierced that idea. It got to me. I now had to think about what I was sublimating or compensating for. That's the context, I don't think you have to look into it more than that.

DD: This happened early in your clinical formation. Do you still get comments like that?

PV: I think it still happens, but on another level. What comes to mind is that in a relatively short period of time, I have been consulted by four mothers who had lost a child. Two of them in very dramatic circumstances. For the time being, I don't think that I could support a fifth. It's not the same as those remarks, but still, it's something that gets to you subjectively. Confrontation with tragedy can be a lot to bear. It is immense. You try to help carry the weight, but it's very overwhelming sometimes.

DD: This interview has been a good start to reflect on the theme a bit, and think about the effect patients have on us. The next interview I have planned is with Stijn Vanheule, as there is one case that he often mentions in his lectures. Have you ever heard him talk about this case in particular?

PV: Yes, that's a good example to elaborate on "Who's your Dora?" as well. The case Stijn discusses shows how a patient's reaction can destabilise your position. Sometimes you are caught up with yourself and your own position.

If you take that destabilisation seriously, it does something to you and you can work with that.

DD: It is something you have to take seriously.

PV: It's your patient pinpointing your own position within the transference. If it gets to you, it's a sign that there is something there. Otherwise, it wouldn't get to you as much. Again: it resonates. Ideally, a comment like that comes early in your career so you can do something with it.

DD: You said it pinpoints a position in the transference?

PV: Exactly, that's what it's about.

DD: I'll bring all of this with me to the next interviews, and see where it takes me. A big thanks for your time and candidness!

PV: With great pleasure.

Notes

1 Verhaeghe, P. (2008 [2005]). *On Being Normal and Other Disorders.* Routledge, New York.
2 Dulsster, D. (2020). *The Process of Lacanian Talking Therapy and its Supervision Considered Closely: A Conceptual-Qualitative Study.* Ghent University, Faculty of Psychology and Educational Sciences.

Chapter 3

Stijn Vanheule – Encountering a Zen-Buddhist Master

Stijn Vanheule is a clinical psychologist and professor of psychoanalysis and clinical psychology at Ghent University (Belgium), where he is the chair of the Department of Psychoanalysis and Clinical Consulting. His research focuses on conceptual discussions in Lacanian psychoanalysis, psychoanalytic and psychodynamic approaches of psychosis, and the critical study of psychological assessment and psychiatric care. He is the author of multiple academic papers and monographs on these topics. Together with Derek Hook and Calum Neill he edited the book series *Reading Lacan's Écrits: From 'Signification of the Phallus' to 'Metaphor of the Subject'*. Stijn Vanheule is also a privately practising psychoanalyst in Ghent, and a member of the New Lacanian School for Psychoanalysis and the World Association of Psychoanalysis.

Dries Dulsster (DD): Dear Stijn, as with all participants, I would first like to thank you for taking part in this project. After Paul Verhaeghe, you are the second in line. One of the reasons I wanted to interview you is because, like Paul, you introduced me to psychoanalysis. Your answer to the question "Who is your Dora?" seems obvious to me, since it is a case study that you often use while teaching, but it is also a case which holds an important place in your book *Why Psychosis is Not So Crazy*,[1] where you talk about your patient Mario, calling him your 'Zen-Buddhist Master'. So, let's talk about Mario's case and the effect it has had on you.

SV: Yes, well, when I had just graduated as a clinical psychologist, I immediately received an opportunity to start working in an institution for people with intellectual disabilities. The institution was located 150 kilometres from Ghent, where I was living at the time. I was given a lot of freedom to do my job how I wanted to. I chose to work on a project to develop outpatient guidance for people with intellectual disabilities and additional psychiatric issues. Since most of these people were residing in an institution or with family, and could not move independently, we always met them where they lived. This also unlocked the opportunity for an individual connection with people in a

DOI: 10.4324/9781003410935-3

population group that is usually hard to reach. There were also mainly group activities in the institution where I worked. This method appealed less to me, because it usually derived from the idea of getting people back on track through a logic of disciplining. So that's how I started this job. It ran parallel with the fact that shortly after graduating I bought the collected works of Freud with my first salary.

DD: With your first paycheck? Yeah, I did that too. Good investment!

SV: Definitely. Since my new job was 150 kilometres from where I was living, I moved to a small village where there was really nothing to do, so I spent my evenings reading Freud's texts. This turned out to be very interesting to me, because I had these clinical encounters going on in parallel. It made what I was reading more concrete. So, I was reading Freud, while working in outpatient counselling, all the while I was also going through my own analysis. During that time, I met Mario, and he taught me so much.

DD: Do tell!

SV: Mario is someone I followed up for a little over a year. I visited him and his parents about fifty times. I of course talked to him during every visit, but I also talked to his parents a lot. When I say 'his parents', I mainly mean his mother. His father was often so emotional that he couldn't really talk. The father sat there, usually with tears in his eyes, after which he went outside to look at his birds, and then stayed outside. From the perspective of my employer, I was free to choose the therapeutic approach. There were no instructions concerning how I should proceed. I could go my own way, and by doing so, by having those meetings, I learned a lot from Mario – not from a great expert, but from someone with an IQ of 35.

DD: Before we discuss Mario any further, maybe you could tell a bit more about his mother, because she seems important to the story.

SV: Mario was 18 when we started our conversations. His mother, however, was in her early 70s. Mario came when she thought she was going through menopause. Nevertheless, she turned out to still be fertile, and they had a child. Their older children had already left home when she fell pregnant with Mario. Obviously, the pregnancy was a shock to this couple. Until I arrived, little had been processed from that shock. Mario developed problems at the age of 18, but it was clear that his mother was also very eager to talk. She was clearly dealing with all sorts of things, and the question she was most concerned with was what would happen to Mario if they could no longer care for him. These were very sweet, very cordial people. Whenever I went there, they always served cake and coffee. At the same time, this cordiality covered a very strong repression.

There's the story of the mother's grief, the grief and terror around the birth of the child, the fact that she didn't really want the child but then was happy he was there after all, and her fear of not knowing if her other children will be taking care of him when they, the parents, will no longer be there. How does his future look? All of this had never been given a place.

I visited to talk to her about her son, but she took the opportunity to talk about herself. After discussing her son's background and context, the conversation turned to her own experiences. As I mentioned earlier, it was mainly the mother who spoke to me, because the father always left the room in an affected manner. I asked him several times to sit down with us, and as long as coffee was drunk or cake was eaten, he was fine. However, as soon as anything subjective came up, he disappeared. What I'm getting at is that there must have been something going on with both parents, but it was the mother specifically who seized the opportunity to start working on several matters.

Mario was always in his sister's old, empty bedroom. His sister had already moved out. He only came down to eat or take a bath, but otherwise he just sat upstairs all day long. Mario sat there on a chair at an old desk with a large stereo and a stack of CDs, his headphones on, and a homemade microphone in his hand. All day long he was listening to Schlager music, mostly Flemish singer Dana Winner. He knew all the lyrics by heart and he always sang along. But he also looked at me anxiously. It was immediately clear that Mario did not know how to carry himself in relation to other people. This bubble of music was his private world. Others could see this world, but they didn't have access to his experiences. The initial complaint formulated by his parents was that he never left his room. Mario went to special education, a type of school for people with severe intellectual disabilities. Remember, he had an IQ of 35, and spoke in two- or three-word sentences. However, he did have an extensive vocabulary in a way. At school he was mainly taught general daily skills, like how to go to the store, how to wash oneself, how to dress, and how to perform light manual labour with the intention of being able to participate in a day centre. By the time they called in for help, he had refused to go to school for six months already. He didn't say it literally, but at 17 he started having huge crying fits and panic attacks. He sometimes threw himself on the floor when he had to get on the bus. Eventually, he wouldn't even leave the room anymore. At some point his parents tried, together with the bus driver, to drag him out of there. His father and mother couldn't handle it anymore. They stood there, crying, together with Mario. Mario then withdrew more and more, which triggered the parents' search for help. Their request was very clear: they wanted him to go back to school, and to be able to reclaim his life.

DD: Mario did not ask for help himself?

SV: No, it was at the request of his parents. A pragmatic request. Of course I didn't know how to make someone go to school either. However, I figured that if he used to go, something probably intervened, which made me want to investigate. I proposed a way of working to which the parents agreed. I was going to talk to Mario and try to connect with him. It was clear to me that there was no point in forcing Mario, but that I also didn't know any tricks in order to make someone leave a room. You can't just leave out cookies to lure him out of there and into the bus. I was introduced with the words: "This is Stijn, and he's here to talk to you." He had taken off his headphones, and I said I came to help him. He then immediately held an internal monologue, mumbling to his shoulder. He looked away and seemingly 'heard' answers, or rather hallucinated answers. It looked like a pantomime, or a performance the parent's thought was funny. They told me he was talking to Daisy. The mom laughed it off and concealed it with motherly love. I immediately figured I needed to dig through this. At the time I didn't yet know how I would go about doing that, but I'd figure it out as I went along. I visited Mario weekly, went upstairs and sat in the room with him. I asked him about his CDs, about Dana Winner, whether he had attended any performances by her yet, and if I could listen to a certain song. He was also a fan of another Flemish singer, Sam Gooris. Mario talked very enthusiastically about those singers, and as such we were interacting. Every now and then, Daisy would say something, and I would systematically ask him what he was hearing, since I couldn't hear it myself. Eventually, he started telling me what Daisy responded. Interesting to know is that his lips were simultaneously articulating what he heard Daisy say.

DD: A form of ventriloquism then, or how should I picture this?

SV: No, the other way around. There was no sound, but you could see his mouth moving. Like a silent playback. He was singing along, but the lyrics were not audible. It looked like what Lacan wrote about the motor-verbal hallucination, which he got from Séglas; the person who hallucinates articulates those signifiers too, but doesn't experience them as their own words. I found that enormously interesting to observe. I had never seen anyone hallucinate like that. I had seen people hallucinating before, but never someone who articulated his own hallucinations. Mario was also a very funny guy. He knew when I was going to come over, because his mother told him in advance, and his room had a view on the driveway, so he saw me coming. I would ring the doorbell, go to his room, knock on the door, and then he would be startled – overly so. It was as if he was participating in amateur theatre. I felt he had a comical talent. By the way, at that time I was reading *Jokes and Their Relation to the Unconscious*[2] by Freud, which led me to assume that a joke says something. So, I suggested to Mario to tell me a joke every time I came over. In return, I would tell him one too. That's how he started telling jokes, and it became clear to me that what he heard in conversations with Daisy was mostly vulgar content. For example, he told jokes about his father's hobby of breeding birds, like: "The bird craps on dad's head." He would then roll over the floor, laughing. He also mentioned "pinch breasts", and then, with his eyes closed, he would be pinching his own breasts, and then curiously looked at my reaction. This 'breast pinching' was also found in his dialogues with Daisy, which made it clear that he was mostly hearing sexual and aggressive content. In fact, it could not have been more classic. The aggressive content was mostly related to his parents, whom he obviously wanted to get more distant from.

DD: What do you mean?

SV: I mean that the themes that shone through the discourse with Daisy were themes that every human being deals with. That was an eye opener for me; it doesn't matter whether you have a mental disability or not, or what your IQ may be – these issues will come into play. He just wasn't being listened to. It needed to be heard, something needed to be done about it, somehow. In the end, the whole thing wasn't about going back to school or not. The conversations showed that something had to be done around sexuality and separation. I also discovered a parallel track: his mother did everything for him. His mother bathed him, dressed him, made his food, made his sandwiches... Although Mario had learned all of this at school, he didn't have to do anything himself at home. Therefore, at some point I told his mother that she was no longer allowed to go into the bathroom with him. His mother complied, and it was very exciting for her. I remember how she talked about the first time she had left him alone in the bathroom. He ran the bath, made a lot of noise for an hour, and when he was done, the bar of soap was completely used up. Washed and dressed he came out of the bathroom. All this time, the mother had tried to overcompensate for her own guilt. Mario was not a wanted child. He had been loved, but not wanted. She became a dominant momma bear, and her cub was not allowed to leave the nest. He showed us her part in his issues by not going out anymore. By having the mom quit doing everything for him, he gained freedom at home – and then other stories came out.

DD: Stories?

SV: At some point the mother told me – somewhat laughingly – that Daisy actually was a TV personality from a series that Mario watched when he was younger. When Daisy appeared on the screen, Mario went to stand in front of the TV to watch her more closely. His parents thought that was very funny. So funny that Mario internalised Daisy. There was no room for sexuality, so he began to have these internal dialogues. Instead of relating to the screen and the image, his sexuality tilted inward in an internal spectacle. He was immersed by the jouissance of the Other. The paternal function, in the sense of creating space for the separation, failed at that point. I tried to articulate a solution by giving room to the 'no'. Or another story was, for example, that when he was a small child walking through the village, he used to visit the girls from the local scouts. He was loved there. But as he got older, he stopped going, perhaps at the point of the awakening of his sexuality. The girls were no longer purely playmates, they became sexualised bodies. He then quit doing everything, including leaving the house. Towards the end of therapy, Mario did go outside again. He went to the bakery or to the butcher's again on his own.

DD: Can you specify how this sexuality was given place?

SV: By giving him the space to articulate this in relation to me, and by me talking about it with his mother. The problem was that sexuality had not been given place in this context. When his mother was able to let go of her own discomfort with her son's sexual body, space was created for him. Her fear of the future left him petrified in the position of a child who is supposed to be asexual. During these conversations, the mother rearranged the phantasmatic position Mario held for her. In doing so, it is important that I discuss a specific anecdote in detail.

DD: The moment you fell?

SV: Yes, because as I am talking, it seems like I had everything under control: I was reading Freud and Lacan, and that resonated with the clinic. Whereas one of the most interesting breakthroughs in his treatment was a failure on my part, a clownish act. At the time I was also participating in a quality care working group in Brussels. My employer delegated me, and I felt honoured that as a 24 year old I could already do something like that. One day I combined this meeting with a home visit, and I first went to see Mario. I had dressed up for the meeting, but it was raining when I arrived at Mario's house, so I parked my car in the driveway and ran to the front door for shelter. However, the path leading there was paved with slippery tiles, so I slipped and fell onto the grass. My nice clothes were all wet. By now we were a few months into counselling, and Mario was the only one who witnessed my fall. I straightened up while cursing, angry with myself that I now had to have a conversation looking like that, and that I also had to go to that meeting in this condition... But, in the meantime, Mario had spontaneously run down the stairs, opened the door, and shouted very loudly: "Stijn fell!" Then his mother came to see me – she was worried. Mario went back inside to get me a large towel. He dabbed my wet shirt with the towel and kept saying "Stijn fell!" over and over again. At that moment I felt like: "Wow, this is something else." It was the first time I had seen him come down. It was also the first time I had seen him take spontaneous action, in the sense that he went and got a towel when it was needed. Up until then, I was always the one who entered his space and tried to connect with him, never the other way around. At that moment he connected with me. I then, fortunately, had the inspiration to remain passive. I was obviously a bit overwhelmed by the fall, but I just let the surprise of his reaction be there, and that created a breakthrough in the transference. I, who had pictured myself as someone who helps people when they have problems, was now in trouble myself. Before that, he was in the position of the fool: he had problems and I came to help. Suddenly I was the fool: the psychologist, with his nice clothes, was covered in mud. It changed something. And, by the way, he made a joke about it. The next time I asked him to tell a joke, he said: "Stijn fell! Haha!" All the other jokes suddenly mattered less. Something appeared in the transference of laughing at me and ridiculing the seriousness I was occupying. Through that event I came to understand what it means to work from the position of the object a, as a place of the waste position. I was literally dirty, but the fact that I didn't correct it in the moment through my ego, that I didn't correct that fall by quickly diving back into the role of 'psychologist' or 'professional', but just listened and observed, had a facilitating function. At that point Mario began to talk more spontaneously to me. He wasn't talking at my request or because he had a problem, but because he wanted to tell me something. That made me realise afterwards that I was now listening from the place of object a.

DD: It's resisting the temptation to take on the role of the professional.

SV: Yes. Obviously, being the professional is the vantage point of counselling. There is someone with a problem. They're looking for a psychologist. And you're in the role of the expert. From the beginning I certainly used the position of the expert with Mario as well, but turned it around to a hysterisation of the discourse. I immediately tried to leave room for the parents and for Mario to speak during my visits, but even if the conversation opened a little, Mario always spoke with inhibitions. His reserve disappeared the moment something happened that showed I was, for a minute, not occupying the hypercontrolled place of knowledge. Something appeared from the order of castration, the order of the lack. Something became possible, because I didn't cover up the castration that was installed through the impact of chance. In that sense, the coincidence has perhaps been fortunate, because I was also ready for it in my own analysis at that point.

DD: The role of the expert is often used to handle anxiety.

SV: Yes, I felt that anxiety from the beginning, in the sense that I didn't know what I would be doing there exactly. I hardly had any experience in working with someone with an intellectual disability or in giving home support, and I hadn't received any training for it either. But I did have an appetite for it. The fear this situation created kept me alert.

DD: It wasn't a paralysing anxiety, but an anxiety that made you work.

SV: Anxiety can prevent a person from making contact, but if you want to find new leads, you have to get past that. I never felt paralysing anxiety during Mario's treatment. I did feel a level of anxiety that went hand in hand with not knowing, because 'knowing' was a safe haven for me as a young clinician. I wanted to know as much as possible. But the clinic of psychoanalysis doesn't work that way. You have to be able to work with 'that-which-you-don't-know', and not fill it in with all sorts of things. That was certainly a point of anxiety for me, but that's where one's own analysis comes in.

DD: I'd like to talk about the relationship to one's own analysis more later, but let's first touch on what seemed to appear spontaneously. When telling your story, you mention the expert position, the place of the object, hysterising... It is Lacan's discourse theory. It's striking.

SV: Yes, indeed. I also indicated something about the master's discourse. I was there, a 24 year old, pointing out to a 72-year-old lady that she, in her own house, was not allowed to enter the bathroom of her son whom she had been caring for for eighteen years...

DD: You see that as master's discourse?

SV: Yes, because it implies an order: 'You can't do that anymore!'

DD: I find it a little strange when we talk about psychoanalysis to say that you make interventions from the master's discourse.

SV: It isn't strange to me. Analytic work rotates through the different discourses. When you tell someone to 'take a seat', that's also the master's discourse. You sit there and I sit here, or you could lie down on the sofa over there. If you want to lie down, we'll talk about it. When you install a framework, you find yourself in the master's discourse, because you don't question it – and you don't explain it either. The master's discourse is all about the rules of the game and the outlines you decide on. Subsequently, hysterisation can occur. When I tell Mario's mother not to go into the bathroom while her son is bathing, I didn't say that as an object *a*. It did stem from the master's discourse, because it's a dictum at that point.

DD: But it's an intervention that you don't just do, right? It comes from an underlying theory.

SV: Yes, from the logic of the case. Nevertheless, in that moment, I am in the master's discourse. For me, in analytic practice, a flash from the master's discourse does appear every now and then. We then observe the effects of the intervention, and tilt back to the analytic discourse. If Mario's mother would have continued to go into the bathroom anyway, I would have needed to figure out another form of containment or way to install limits.

DD: I remain a bit confused. That which propels the master is his hidden truth. In the university's discourse it concerns the hidden theory or dogma's, the Freudian–Lacanian theory for example. Surely it is the latter that orients your interventions.

SV: I see it rather as the master's discourse, because there's an act going on that erases my own subjective decision. I don't have rock-solid evidence to make such an intervention. It is a decision that expresses what I think is best, which is always a normative point. And because of that normativity, I would say it's the master's discourse. If I would have told the mother that it is important for Mario to stand on his own two feet, and if I would have explained transitions in young adulthood to her, then I would have presented a psychological story – and that would have been the university's discourse.

DD: So that is something you can use as well.

SV: Yes, but also as a flash, as a construction that you insert but immediately let go of again. It is always an intervention that, at best, moves someone and invites them to continue speaking and searching. An impetus to hysterisation, in other words.

DD: So, concerning the interaction with one's own analysis... When I was drawing the initial outlines of this book and talking to people about the theme, someone commented that the formative effect of clinical work was irrelevant, and that the focus should be on one's own analysis. I have a hard time agreeing with that comment.

SV: One's own analysis is important, but it's separate from clinical work. I don't think you can take on the position of the analyst solely based on your own analysis. It's about meeting others and being ready for a certain type of encounter, where neither your ego, nor your views, nor your knowledge are in the foreground, nor is anxiety allowed to take over. There are definitely clinical moments and patients that shape you as an analyst. It is important to merge both, because you don't learn how to swim in a puddle on your desk. Lacan, for example, undoubtedly learned a lot from his encounter with Aimée. It shaped him in how he took the story of psychotic patients seriously. Freud, on the other hand, ran into the issue of psychosis.

DD: It reminds me of a remark of the late Prof. Filip Geerardyn, who stated in one of his lectures that there are four important pillars in becoming an analyst: one's own analysis, supervision, cartels, and working with psychosis. The first three can also be found in Freud, but the last one surprised me. I think I panicked at the time: "What if I will never have the chance to work with psychosis?" In the meantime, I have come to understand what he meant. In addition to confronting oneself in one's own analysis, there are also clinical encounters. Now, you call Mario your Zen-Buddhist Master. In his first seminar, Lacan refers to this Zen-Buddhist Master with the statement that this master provides an answer at exactly the moment when the student is ready for the answer. Could you perhaps tell me a little more about that?

SV: Mario was not a master as in the discourse of the university. He was not concerned with theories and intellectual debates. For me, he was a Zen-Buddhist Master, because with very few words he made it clear to me in which place it was best to position myself. Being verbal is sometimes more like a cloud, a fog... speaking and speaking and speaking... He didn't have that much to say, but what he said was relevant. I am someone who speaks easily and who likes to speak. He had fewer words, but he still made me understand that you have to be able to work with lack, that you have to work from the object *a* position. You should not inflate your ego. You have to let go and be present with your full body, both of your ears, and the words you have available. When you are sufficiently present as an empty space, the other person begins to relate to that space from their specific problems. That is what I understood through him.

DD: An important remark that Paul Verhaeghe received from his analysand was whether he was compensating or sublimating during his sessions. It reminds me of that.

SV: It's about a presence in clinical practice, separate from the ego, separate from ideals, separate from the image of what I think is important and what is going to work. Mario made that clear to me. As a student I surrounded myself with intellectuals. They were present physically and in the books I read. The idea of 'the intellectual' was an ideal that appealed to me. I was also attracted to the idea that an analyst is someone who studies thoroughly. Therefore, I started reading Freud's collected works. I read these based on the idea that I could do something with it. And it helped in the sense that Freud made the ethics about listening and speaking clear to me. But at that stage it was still theoretical knowledge that of course echoed with my own analysis. Importantly, my encounter with Mario worked as a sort of purification that showed it was not about intellectual knowing. In my analysis, working with Mario helped me to deconstruct my own ego and to become more present during clinical work. It taught me to focus on 'being there for the Other', for what is different, rather than always wanting to know. Mario taught me that performing, being the best, and looking good, none of those things matter. The only thing that benefits from this outwardly performance is my opinion about myself, but it doesn't benefit anyone else. I was undoubtedly working through that at the time in my own analysis, because around that time, this understanding also shifted in my own life. At one point there was someone in the psychoanalytic society who said to me that he didn't recognise me anymore, that I used to always be serious, very restrained, taking notes and discussing. He didn't know that I could let my hair down as well. His remark came as a surprise to me, but at the same time it was not surprising at all. There used to be something restrained, intellectualised about me, which also marked my psychology studies. My grades were excellent, but my extreme devotion was neurotic. The encounter with Mario demonstrated how this was changing through analysis. That literal fall made the idea that my clinical practice would revolve around my achievements and accolades disappear like snow in the sun.

DD: On the intellectual aspect, it did strike me in the interview with Paul that his clinical encounters had an impact on his theoretical elaborations, such as the aspect of actual pathology. You have several books on psychosis. In one of them, Mario is clearly discussed. You have also written a book on diagnostics. Did clinical encounters play a role in this?

SV: I was already interested in psychosis before that. In my analysis, I did manage to trace the origins of this interest to a family history. My grandfather's aunt murdered all her children while she was pregnant. She probably – I can say this in retrospect – had a psychotic crisis during her fourth or fifth pregnancy, and killed her offspring out of desperation. She was then locked up in jail, and she took her own life after her last child was born. It was taboo to talk about any of it in my family. I had only heard it be vaguely mentioned as a child. People said that she was crazy, but as soon as I asked for more information, my grandmother told me to 'shut up'. My mother didn't know much about it either. When I worked through this story in my own analysis, it also became clear to me where my interest in psychosis came from, and why I wanted to read Lacan's *Seminar III: The Psychosis*[3] first. In other words, I was interested in psychosis because within my family we weren't allowed to talk about any of it. And the desire to talk about psychosis was an effect of my analysis. This fascination has certainly driven me to study psychosis more, but, at the same time, I also had to work through this fascination. My encounter with Mario had a part in this process. My fascination has made room for an interest in talking about psychosis instead. We're not going to be silent about psychosis. We're not going to leave it to the discourse of power and pure medicalisation. We're not going to dehumanize people with psychosis. The patients and families who are dealing with psychosis should also be heard. It *can* be talked about, and I see it as my task to help encourage an open discourse. People should be able to talk about their own psychotic experiences or the psychoses of their children. They should have that space. We shouldn't treat them as if they are 'special'.

Mario could still hear Daisy after our sessions had come to an end. So what? He did leave his house again, but he still didn't want to go to school. A day centre where he could work was fine by him. To explore that option I visited a day centre together with him. There he started talking to Daisy at a certain point. His unconscious spoke to him in the form of an open dialogue, not through the return of the repressed. But without going through my own analysis, I wouldn't have been able to work with Mario in the way that I did. I don't know if my relationship to psychosis would have been the same without Mario. I think meeting Mario was significant in many ways.

I could also have talked to you about the first analysands in my private practice, because I also collided with psychosis in that context, but this happened years after I had met Mario. However, these analysands also stimulated formative moments for me. Two analysands come to mind immediately in this regard.

DD: Could you tell me something about them as well?

SV: There is one case where I learned a lot about the role of diagnostics. In the course of that treatment I changed my diagnosis several times. I started working from the perspective of neurosis, so to speak, though later I realised that what this person was saying was absolutely not neurotic. I then decided on the hypothesis of psychosis for a while, only to get to a point where I wasn't sure anymore whether it was about psychosis at all. I thought it also could have been neurosis. Eventually, I decided that a psychotic logic was central here. This process was interesting for me, because it was spread out over several years and it made me look at diagnosis in a totally different way.

DD: What do you mean?

SV: It showed me that psychoanalytic diagnostics is not about a set psychological reality that is an ingrained and immovable element. No! Psychoanalytic diagnostics is about the structure of transference, and the place that the unconscious obtains in transference. In the case I talked about, I changed my mind three times about the diagnosis, and each time it led me to a different position in transference – albeit with caution, because it was clear that I shouldn't be interpreting too much. It confronted me with the incredible normality that can characterise psychosis, and with the relative difference from neurosis. For example, there is indeed less normativity in the Oedipal organisation, so there is less of a compass to orient oneself in relation to others. But relationships with the other can be lavishly present, and hold a challenge in how one deals with children, a partner, or parents. This challenge characterises psychosis as much as neurosis. The difference is that in neurosis there is, in one way or another, an 'actually it has to be this way' answer ready. It is a construction, an answer built on one's own Oedipal history, resulting in all the internal contradictions that characterise neurosis. This radical awareness has helped me to listen carefully. Switching between diagnoses also allowed me to ask different questions and to listen differently.

DD: You said you immediately thought of two analysands?

SV: The other case taught me a lot about fundamental fantasy. With Mario I learned to understand object *a* as a waste position, with this analysand it occurred to me that object *a* can also be the voice and the gaze. I also learned how someone can evolve in that respect through analysis. First this analysand heard the voice of his conscience resonate strongly, and then he started incarnating the voice itself in certain contexts. The voice can circulate as object *a* and then return in dreams, childhood memories, preoccupations – all kinds of things. I learned about object *a* in neurosis beyond the signifiers of neurosis. In my own analysis, I was, at first, more in touch with the unconscious, but less with where I was situating the object *a*. It is by noticing this movement in analysands that I became able to question it for myself.

DD: So, it was through these experiences in your clinical practice that you were able to take steps in your own analysis as well?

SV: Clinical practice has always had that impact on me. I've also always dreamed about my patients and analysands. Encounters like this enter the unconscious and transform who you are, which in turn has an impact on your encounters. When working intensely with someone, you see them more often than many of your friends and family members. The stories you're told touch jouissance. So also my jouissance. Sometimes it keeps me awake, sometimes it makes me dream. In other words, my work enters my unconscious, it touches my jouissance, and along the way it definitely influences my own analysis.

DD: Those are indeed different encounters than those with Mario.

SV: Yes. Those two later cases were people with a much bigger vocabulary. What was so interesting with Mario, is that he didn't have a treasure chest of signifiers – it was more like a small wallet. But he managed to play the game with his coins as well. You can have a treasure chest with lots of signifiers, but that makes the game rather opaque in certain areas. In Mario's case, everything was out in the open. Actually, another thing I learned through Mario is the importance of the style with which he was dealing with me – that foolishness he developed.

DD: You mean being funny?

SV: Yes, being funny towards me. His awkwardness when socialising transformed into a foolish way of doing things, which allowed him to connect. I also observed that it was pointless to think about how he *should* behave, while he had found something that worked for him. As time went on, I also saw him interacting more jokingly with his parents. Before that, he was rather withdrawn and scared. In his foolishness appeared a sinthome – distilled from the dialogues, encounters, follies, and incidents that characterised him – with which he manifested his individuality. From there, Mario invented the style of the slightly nonchalant, awkwardly joking guy.

DD: Concerning those incidents… it's pure contingency.

SV: Yes, I agree. It's daring to allow contingency to play its role, and I think that this is where us being analysts comes into play. We don't classify contingency into categories of 'this is it' and 'I have to read that this way', or 'he's making that kind of comment now', and 'that's a dream of this type'. I didn't know what to do with Mario, but I did learn to allow contingency. It really is a big piece of our clinical work, and I learned to understand this through, among others, Mario.

DD: A Zen-Buddhist Master indeed. Thanks a lot for the interview!

SV: You're welcome. My pleasure.

Notes

1 Vanheule, S. (2021). *Waarom een Psychose niet zo Gek is* [*Why a Psychosis is Not So Crazy*]. Lannoo Campus.
2 Freud, S. (1960 [1905]). *Jokes and Their Relation to the Unconscious. Standard Edition*, VIII, The Hogarth Press, London.
3 Lacan, J. (1981 [1955–1956]). *Le Séminaire III: Les Psychoses*. Seuil, Paris.

Chapter 4

Evi Verbeke – Theory to Practice

Evi Verbeke is a psychologist and psychoanalyst who did a PhD on power and ethics in contemporary psychiatry. Currently, she works as a guest professor at the University of Ghent (Department of Psychoanalysis and Clinical Consulting), as a psychologist at an assisted living facility for people with mental health problems, and also has a private practice. She is the author of *Psychiatrie op Drift* (translation: *Psychiatry Adrift: On Power, Ethics and Resistance* (2024)).

Dries Dulsster (DD): Let me start by thanking you for wanting to participate in this project.

Evi Verbeke (EV): Gladly!

DD: After the interview with Paul Verhaeghe and Stijn Vanheule, I thought it would be fun to dialogue about clinical encounters with a peer, someone who has had a similar trajectory in psychology and psychoanalysis. You and I started studying psychology together in 2005, we both did our post-graduate training, and we each started to work on a PhD after this. As such, I think it is only logical to include you in this book, and I'm very glad you accepted. So, the question the interviews start with is: "Who is your Dora?"

EV: I immediately think of two people. Someone from my private practice, and someone I've seen in an institutional context. But I wonder whether I should pick cases that taught me something about psychoanalysis or about what psychoanalysis actually is. Or are you interested in Dora in the sense of a case where, as was the case for Freud and Dora, one harshly stumbles on personal issues. The case of Dora is a case study Freud continued to work on, while asking himself what had actually happened there. He drew some lessons from it. With 'the young homosexual woman',[1] we see a totally different Freud appear. So, there are two ways to go about this question.

DD: Everyone gets to decide for themselves how they interpret the question and what cases they want to discuss.

DOI: 10.4324/9781003410935-4

EV: Everyone who comes to speak to me teaches me something about psychoanalysis, but let's talk about a case of someone who was one of my first patients in my private practice. This is a woman who gave me a stronger transference to psychoanalysis. She had been referred to me by a facility for people with mental disabilities. She had an IQ of 50. She couldn't read. She couldn't write. Though she did live alone in a small apartment. She also worked at that facility. I have discussed this case in several supervisions, and once in a cartel during our postgraduate training – you were there too. This woman was in therapy with me for about three years. She came to see me once a week, and for a short period of time twice a week. One of the guidance counsellors described her over the phone as someone who kept repeating the same pattern in her life. She was together with a very sweet, gentle man, but she couldn't have sex with him. She couldn't, even though she wanted to. At some point she started to cheat on her boyfriend, usually in a fairly violent, aggressive manner, and it was always accompanied by a lot of misery. It had happened again right before contacting me; she had run away with a man, ended up in the woods, and was left there, alone, without knowing how to get back home. The question was whether she had been abused or not. There were doubts about it, but what was certain was that he had left her there. Her guidance counsellor indicated that things like this had happened a lot, so she asked me if I could give this woman psychoeducation about sexuality. This question startled me greatly. Because she had a mental disability, her symptom was immediately interpreted as a lack of knowing – unrelated to any psychological dynamics. They wanted me to fill in the blanks by giving her technical knowledge. But I didn't go into it further during this phone call. They also told me that it was a woman with a very traumatic past, and that she had probably experienced abuse at home. I simply responded that she could come over. Our first conversation took place with her guidance counsellor present. She didn't say much herself, but she did ask me at one point: "If I come to you, can you make sure that it works out between my boyfriend and me?" So there *was* a question present, and it is why I thought she would keep coming to see me. But the second session she didn't show up. I didn't have her phone number, so I didn't know how to reach her, but I thought that she might have forgotten, or maybe her appointment wasn't properly relayed to her by the facility. When I called the facility to see what was going on, they were very angry. They told me that she had run away – "Again!" Shortly after, they called me back saying: "She left, and then she told us that she couldn't find your practice. Then she went to get a coffee." They said it was impossible for her not to find my practice, since she knows the neighbourhood very well: "We don't believe it, she ran away!" I thought: "Yeah, well, that can happen. Better luck next time." It never happened again afterwards, but the whole ordeal really stuck with me because of these words that, especially in the early sessions, came up a lot: 'running away'. That's how both she and her guidance counsellor named the incident. 'Running away' was something this woman used often during later sessions as well. She had 'run away' from her lover, her mother had 'run away' from the family, her sister had 'run away' from her father. It was a phrase that was repeated a lot. It was only in supervision that I realised that this 'running away' was immediately present in the transference. That's how she referred to it: "I didn't want to run away from you." I found it striking that this symptom came up so quickly in the transference. After several conversations, it also became clear that she had absolutely no lack of knowledge about sexuality. She knew all too well what it was all about! She herself was also morally distorted by the fact that she could not sleep with her lover. She really wanted to. But at the same time, she was cheating on him. She was distraught over that too. She is someone who very readily came to a form of classical analytical speech, in the sense that she was associating, discussing dreams, and that none of it was meaningless to her. She was implicated in her own speech. She taught me that I wanted to understand things far too quickly. For example, she had many nightmares about spiders crawling all over her, and I quickly sexualised that. But my remark left her indifferent. Much later she recounted a memory of where she was sitting on a dirty toilet at her grandmother's house. Her grandparents were unhygienic people. This toilet was outside, where the floor was covered in spiders. She told me she wasn't afraid of the spiders at the time, but that the door had blown open and the neighbours could now see her sitting on the toilet. After sharing this memory out loud, this particular nightmare no longer occurred. At the end, she even said she no longer had that dream altogether. She did not say that this nightmare had disappeared because her memory had been turned into speech, but rather that she was rid of the nightmare. The fact that she could put things into speech had much more effect than me saying something like: "The spiders crawling all over you." She had other dreams too, especially about her mother who had left the family when she was young, and about her aunt for whom she had a specific name – her 'for-real-mother'. Her aunt had died, and she had many dreams about her passing. In her dreams, this for-real-mother often sternly said: "What are you doing now?!" She was somewhat impressed by the aunt's judgement. A judgement that was obviously still there. I didn't realise until much later how central the aunt's gaze was in all those matters. She also shared another memory during the first session with the guidance counsellor, and she talked more about it later. This memory was first a bit disjointed, but later it gained consistency. After her mother had run away from the family, the analysand lived with her father. The latter owned a bar, and she recounted that one night when her father was away, she was alone with her older sister. Her father had said that if he was not there, the bar would not be open. But her sister *did* open the bar, and let all the men in. Then, her sister laid down on the pool table, and "did what men and women do to each other, with all those men. I saw all of that." She likewise related that "father used to creep in with sister at night, and I had to watch all of that." I'm a little embarrassed to say it now, but in the beginning, I sometimes thought: "That's so terrible for your sister! Why are you so hung up on this 'I had to see all that'?" Fortunately, I was able to distance myself from that thought, and I questioned myself through analysis and supervision.

DD: The case clearly illustrates the level of the signifier, being the 'running away', and then the level of the object, being the gaze.

EV: Yes, it's a case that was very illustrative. I think that's why it has stayed with me like this. It's a case I've thought about and discussed a lot, and it's also the first case I've talked about publicly. Maybe every case is equally illustrative, but this case pushed me to think about what happens in the analytic space. I was paddling in the great analytic lake, and this woman pushed me under water. But I'm still swimming, occasionally drowning, and then floating back up again. Analysis and supervision are important tools for that. In the case of this woman – especially through supervision – it became clear to me that something of the gaze was at play. The phantasmatic image of 'a woman being reduced to an object by a man while someone watches', was a scene that recurred in many of her stories and dreams. There was a memory where she had seen a teacher fiddling with a girl. She was always more like a passive-active spectator of something that was happening and that completely turned in her current relationship to the Other. Now, as an adult, she's no longer just watching, but she's reducing herself to the object of a man. In the process, there was always someone watching as well. For example, she once walked hand in hand with a man at the market, while her boyfriend saw what was going on. Or whenever she cheated, her guidance counsellor found out what had occurred. All these instances didn't strike me as 'stupidity', but as part of staging the phantasm – which was also entirely part of her play, though her position had changed. It wasn't until I started to write about this case – as opposed to just talking about it – that some of these things became clear to me, and I could form a certain clinical logic. That's how she taught me something about psychoanalysis: we don't judge, we construct a logic. We don't get stuck in an idea of 'we know too little' or 'what the hell is she doing?' We operate from a certain logic, and only then can your ego or jouissance remain out of the equation.

DD: What do you mean by that?

EV: When I said just now that I thought it was strange at first that she referred to herself as a victim when her sister was the one being abused, that's an example of how my own ego came into play. I was listening to those particular memories from my own frame of mind, and therefore I didn't understand a thing. For me, the great value of psychoanalysis lies in it being a framework that allows us to put our ego aside, and listen to the dynamics of a singular patient. We listen to it in such a way that we don't dismiss a patient's actions as behaviour that someone displays purely intentionally. It concerns behaviour of a speaking human being who is essentially divided. And it is in that division that we hypothesise about the logic of a case. In this woman's case, supervision helped me to step away from my own moral bias while listening to what was at stake. Only then could I theorise the function of the gaze within this case. Only then could I hear her pleasure and her fear in those scenes, and she, in turn, could speak freely and seek a different relationship towards what had happened. She might never have been able to afford that freedom if I had remained stuck with my initial feelings. Psychoanalysis says that we should not apply our theory *linea recta* to our patients. That is absolutely true, but some people mistake that guideline for the idea that theory is secondary. Theory helps us to hear people's subjective divisions, and not dismiss their speech and behaviour as 'difficult', 'not ok', or 'they're doing it to themselves'. Theory allows us to see people as subjects who don't coincide with themselves; they do silly things they have no control over, or they desire something, but then do the opposite… As a clinician it gives you an ear for those incongruities, and at the same time a certain humility. Your own personal ideas just matter less.

DD: I wanted to follow up on your comment that working with this woman had the effect of being 'more' into psychoanalysis. It implies that there was a transference to psychoanalysis (EV: Yes!), but also that this case had the effect of increasing this transference, so to speak. Could you say a little bit more about that?

EV: I think it gave me the belief that psychoanalysis can work.

DD: You didn't have that belief before?

EV: I did, but it was more of an abstract belief. Psychoanalysis *had* to work, because those professors I looked up to said it works. But that wasn't enough for me. Through this case study, this faith was lived through and revitalised. I believed it, because I saw in my clinical practice what effects psychoanalytic work can have on a person. What I had read before now appeared in what I was doing with a patient. Though it remains a matter of belief. It is not a certainty that psychoanalysis works; I cannot firmly assert how an analysis will turn out for everyone. It is an act of faith, as Lacan also noted, in which you will sometimes take a certain position. With this woman it became clearer to me how the analytical position can trigger something in a patient. By letting her speak, and by giving her the space to express her subjective division, she was able to elaborate on a memory of which she only had bits and pieces left. And by suspending my own judgement, it became possible to manoeuvre in the transference as well – and something changed within this woman. For example, she could later say that she looked at her sister and thought: "I actually want to be hugged too." Or she realised: "Oh, my mom and my sister had a lot of men, but actually, so did I." Through speaking, she became involved in a story that she had previously been mostly a victim of. I actually thought that was a huge effect, especially in someone who was seen as limited and not able to do much. All the more so because then a lot changed in her relational life, her nightmares disappeared, and she talked to people about her difficulties differently than before. These effects were still there years after the therapy, which I was told when, by coincidence, I encountered her guidance counsellor again. That a certain effect could be achieved by having someone speak and listen in a certain way, made me feel that psychoanalysis does work. It doesn't work the same way for everyone, but it did give me confidence in the idea that if you follow the logic of the case and take an analytical position, things will change. The prerequisite, however, is that you have to speak about your patients in supervision, and that you elaborate on your own case a little further in your own analysis. That the therapy had such an effect on this particular woman surely increased my transference to psychoanalysis.

DD: It also started with a woman of whom they assumed a lack of knowledge concerning sexuality, and concluded she needed psychoeducation. And you figured she did have knowledge, but in a different way. That's that act of faith?

EV: Yes. It is about the belief that every human being, regardless of their cognitive ability or pathology, is a 'subject' in the Lacanian sense. It is not because someone cognitively knows less, or is less self-reliant, that they have no unconscious, no desire, no pleasure, and that they cannot bear witness to that somehow, in any way. Every human being desires, dreams, enjoys, fantasises, does not want to know, and desires to know at the same time. But as I say this, I realise that I have not always held that position myself, and it is perhaps precisely for that reason that I choose this – not very classic – case study. When I started my internship, I mainly wanted to provide one-on-one therapy, preferably concerning neurosis, with fairly intelligent people. That was what psychoanalysis was to me at the time. I only later realised that it was because I imagined or fantasized that the professor I looked up to and who had introduced me to psychoanalysis, Paul Verhaeghe, worked like that. Of course, his teachings on actual pathology completely contradicted this image, but at the time, I couldn't imagine working in any other way than the classic one-on-one set-up. This started changing during the year I did my internship, when I heard another professor, Stijn Vanheule, speak about his practice with people with mental disabilities and psychosis. I remember thinking: "Psychoanalysis, that's for everyone." Also, the classes I took on institutional work that year, and the conversations I had with fellow students who were doing internships in less typical places – like *La Borde, Le Courtil,* and *L'antenne 110* – changed my perception of what psychoanalysis is. The one-on-one setting with well-behaved neurotic, intelligent people suddenly felt like a rather limited setting, and I began to feel a lack in my own internship. This remained when I started working. The woman I just discussed, and the work I had started in psychiatry made me overthink psychoanalysis, because both situations taught me in a personal way – and not through what someone else had told me – that psychoanalysis can indeed work for everyone, and that everyone is a subject of the unconscious. I learned that psychoanalysis is not a matter of technique, but that technique is fluid and secondary to an ethic and to listening to the human being as someone with an unconscious mind. So, the difference between psychoanalysis and applied psychoanalysis became superfluous for me.

DD: You refer to supervision or analysis… one's own unconscious is also touched in a certain way.

EV: It reminds me of my intuitive thought: "That must have been bad for you sister." It's good that I discussed this thought in my own analysis. This is also why I find Lacanian psychoanalysis so interesting when it comes to counter-transference. Of course, there is countertransference; we won't deny that from a Lacanian perspective. Nobody is a blank computer screen. But we need to ask what to do with this countertransference. If you discuss this in your own analysis, it offers an opening to start listening to someone in a different way. Your own unconscious no longer gets in the way. Another instance where I behaved in my typical manner was my revolt to the guidance counsellor's request to explain sexuality to this patient. From a psychoanalytic perspective, we listen to someone in a different way. That is also why I chose to study psychoanalysis, and it is important to me, but it likewise returned in the transference. With this lady, judgement was very central in the beginning of the sessions. She was often saying things to me, like: "I'm not allowed to do that, right Evi?" After a while it became clear to her that I wasn't judging what she was telling me, and that I didn't care who she was or wasn't sleeping with. I wasn't there to judge. And this realisation was crucial for her, so that she could feel comfortable to talk everything through. For example, her counsellors had told me "She shouldn't talk too much about her past", that she "had to confess to her partner that she had cheated on him". I then told the institution that I found this to be an ethical issue. Everyone there figured that confessing to him made sense, but I told them: "70 per cent of people sometimes cheat on their partners, but not all of them have counsellors who demand to confess." Everyone shuffled their feet a bit, but my comment did have an effect. The counselling staff turned it down a notch afterwards. The patient herself quickly realised that I suspended all judgement, but in turn she started to judge the counselling staff during our sessions: "They shouldn't say that, right, Evi? They aren't allowed to do that, are they, Evi?" What I intuitively wanted to say was: "Ah yes, those counselors... they don't have a clinical compass... What are they doing!" But fortunately, I realised quickly enough that her remarks were a trap. It can be important for some patients to hear me say something like: "It's rubbish what that person has said!" But I certainly could not do that in her case, I had to handle it more carefully. How people with disabilities are treated is a sensitive issue for me. How are they perceived? Do they have the right to exist on their own? Are they given choices? Still, I had to make sure I didn't go along with judging the guidance counsellors, even though that would have been my spontaneous reaction. However, it would not have been interesting to collude against and judge the counsellors. Again, this meant a reversal of positions.

DD: It's interesting how discussing the countertransference in one's own analysis creates the opening to start listening to someone differently. Was that how it went with the other case as well?

EV: The other one also connects to what I just talked about. This case concerns a boy from an institution who made me think: "I don't want to work like that." The way the institution had treated this boy was irreconcilable with psychoanalysis for me. It is through this boy that I quickly realised I wanted to work in an institution using a psychoanalytic frame. I wanted to do it like that, or I wouldn't do it at all. He was 16 when he was first admitted. His family were carnival workers, which was perceived by our team as chavvy. His father was no longer in the picture, but he was very close with his mother and his brother. However, the team felt that their bond was 'too much', and thought they should be somewhat pulled apart. They thought it was too symbiotic. But I thought: "That may be the case, but who are we to pull mother and son apart?" This was not how I wanted to work with people. Their regard also appeared in how they referred to him: "He does have some psychopathic traits, no?" I tried to counter that, and said that we should absolutely not make statements like that about a 16 year old. So, in my book,[2] I described an incident where he had been put in seclusion for something stupid. I was still there in the evening, and a colleague gave me the phone and said: "It's his mother, she wants to talk to him, and you have to tell her that she can't while he is in seclusion." This confinement lasted for twenty-four hours in total. That was the rule. So, I played my role as a psychologist, and said that she could neither hear nor see her son right now. The mother started crying, and I thought: "Evi, what are you doing? You are participating in something you absolutely cannot identify with." I felt very bad when I went home that night. I was wondering why I had gone along with it. I felt the same way another time, when the nurse had spoken very harshly to the mom during a family discussion with that same boy. I just sat there, and let it happen. I asked myself why I hadn't done anything. At the time, I was also working for a leisure organisation in another city. This boy I am talking about wanted to join some of the activities there – we had first met in that organisation – to go and see what they had to offer. I had given him my cell phone number, but he had lost it. He had then contacted the department to ask for my number again, but they replied that they couldn't give out staff numbers, and I got reprimanded. I hadn't given it much thought, as my number could be found online. Anyone could've gotten the number of my private practice. I didn't understand why they were so worked up about that. Afterwards, I didn't really know what my attitude towards him should be. It was someone who didn't give much to work with. He didn't talk much, because he didn't agree with being there. I could sit there and listen to him, but I felt it didn't do much. There was a huge distance between us. But that distance, I think, was perpetuated by our attitude towards him and his mother. The department was not receptive to his suffering. They didn't read his behaviour properly, the idea of an unconscious logic was ignored, and everything he did was seen as intentional and a harbinger of psychopathy. It is impossible for the patient to speak when placed in that position. Anyone who excludes the idea of the unconscious cannot expect the patient to work on their suffering. He was actually a sensitive, vulnerable guy – which I tried to point out to the team. I came to a point where I knew I was going to have to make a choice. I could either stay, but start working differently, or leave. By the way, I wasn't the only one who had a hard time with what was going on. Others were also questioning whether we were doing the right thing with that boy, and what we had gotten ourselves into. There weren't many problems between that mom and that boy. School, however, had a lot of problems with him, because he didn't want to go anymore. Fine, I get that. But why did we need to come between this mother and this boy, when they experienced so few problems between them? And why couldn't anyone be bothered to really listen to the boy, instead of immediately dismissing him as a psychopath?

DD: How did you manage to continue working with that team? Did something shift?

EV: Concerning him, not much. That's also why this case has really stuck with me. It's even different than with Dora. With Dora, Freud was doing his thing as he was blinded by his own view of femininity and psychoanalysis. It's different in institutional work.

DD: Here the team was blinded by their own views, their own ideas.

EV: Indeed. The team had a clear idea about the case: a possibly psychopathic young man who had a symbiotic bond with his mother. As a result, they wanted to nip his behaviour in the bud, and reduce the bond between mother and son. That idea came about, I think, because there wasn't enough framework to work with. We were dealing with a boy who had behavioural problems, and the school was asking us to help resolve them, even though the boy himself had no requests. Well, if you don't have a framework to work with, then you'll easily label his behaviour as 'bad' or 'manipulative' – which then leads to a cruel treatment, such as locking the boy in seclusion for twenty-four hours because he contradicted himself, or commanding his mother to contact her son less. This indeed blinded the team to other issues, such as this boy's talents, his fear of growing up, the pain in that family after the dad had left. For me, psychoanalysis can help in cases like this. With psychoanalysis, it becomes possible to make a case construction of such a boy, to inscribe him in a story. That doesn't mean you'll figure out what is going on exactly, but it will prompt new ideas and insights. As a result, several questions can surface, like: 'What makes him lash out at others?' or 'What symptoms did this family invent to cope, after the father left?' We needed more of these kinds of questions and this kind of thinking. We should've assumed that he is not a bad boy, but someone divided in his suffering. I think this way of working blinds one much less.

DD: When we studied psychology together, it was clear that you were interested in psychoanalysis. It's kind of remarkable to hear that it was a case that had the effect of "Yes, psychoanalysis!" Concerning the first case you discussed, you said: "Yes, more psychoanalysis!" It seems to indicate that we're not there yet with just a transference on psychoanalytic theory.

EV: Yes, it was the experience that it works, and the realisation that if you don't have that framework to lean on, you don't know what to do. That's not to say that I told my team that they should all start reading Lacan. As a matter of fact, it reminds me of a night nurse who had told management: "I suspect Evi is engaging in psychoanalysis." Fortunately, the management laughed and said: "She is being trained in psychoanalysis, we knew that in advance!" To work clinically, you need a framework. Many people talk to me about my book and social workers tell me what is going on in psychiatric wards. They see things that are not right. However, they don't really know what to make of it, or what to do about it. For me, psychoanalysis offers something to hold on to. It gives us a framework for thinking about clinical practice, and for how we should handle the people who come to us and who are, for example, in compulsory treatment. Psychoanalysis will not determine what to do in a specific case, but it does provide a frame of reference for how we can perceive people. What we should avoid is just labelling a 16 year old as antisocial, and write down that he will never be okay. It was the funfair that fascinated him and that worked for him. The question that should have been asked is where he was suffering, instead of where we were suffering in dealing with him. This viewpoint is a totally different way of looking at people. In the end, this outlook did resonate with the employees of the institution where the boy was staying at. Without this framework, I felt adrift in psychiatry. And it is precisely this lack of direction that I often see institutional caregivers struggle with as well. A lot is happening, they need to work at a very high pace, and then they join a team that condemns people or keeps up with a strict approach. If you don't have a framework such as psychoanalysis, you can feel that how the caregivers have to work is not okay, but you have little to counterbalance their approach – and before you know it, you get dragged into it. Psychoanalysis is not the only framework, but it gives the opportunity to ethically ask the right questions, and to find a stance in clinical work. It meant we could think together as a team: 'Let's think about it, what does he say to you? What don't we understand? What is their history? What works for them, and what destabilises them?' We were able to develop case constructions and that proved to be a powerful tool for our team in working with patients. I needed help with that, too. I had my own supervision. After some team meetings on Friday mornings, I had to recover or felt upset. I would then call a friend to talk about it. This one time a friend responded: "Shouldn't you be doing this with your team?" This mostly happened during the first six months, then it calmed down. But I really did need externs for a while.

DD: Could you tell me a bit more about the choice for psychoanalysis?

EV: Yes, for many students in Ghent, the choice for psychoanalysis falls within their education at university. Suddenly you hear something about psychoanalysis, and it grabs a certain group of people. But being gripped by psychoanalysis isn't enough. You can continue to work theoretically, that's also fine, but in order to go further as a therapist and then as an analyst, there has to be another kind of encounter. A clinical encounter. Of course, that's a choice you make. I could also have chosen to leave that clinic instead. I actually almost did. I had another job that I enjoyed a lot. For a moment I considered leaving that institution for the other, more 'fun' job. That would have been easier. On the other hand, some people say: "Psychoanalysis is interesting, but what's the point? In practice, there you are, handling annoying 16year olds who rob people and get angry. We handle these kids by putting them in seclusion." Or someone else once said to me: "I learned a lot from your courses, but I'm in the forensic service, we can't do much with it." Isn't that unfortunate? Of course, you can work with psychoanalysis forensically. There is always something of yourself in it. You can make a choice. You don't have to go along with a rigid system based on punishment, reward, and coercion; psychoanalysis offers a way – even for forensics – to enable a different way of listening, and a different clinic.

DD: There are also those who, at that moment, choose to give up clinical work altogether. I remember Paul Verhaeghe once said in a lecture: "Either they flee into teaching, or they flee into management positions."

EV: Or they flee to another sector. I feel you hear that a lot. The encounter with jouissance in the clinic can be very raw, both the jouissance of mental suffering and the jouissance of care itself. And then many people run away indeed. Or they don't find enough to hold onto in psychoanalysis, and opt for very concrete and goal-oriented therapies instead. There is nothing wrong with any of those other orientations or options or other forms of therapy. But sometimes these fail because the real rears its head – which it always does sooner or later – and then there is the risk that, for example, social workers will respond with seclusion, ending the treatment… Psychoanalysis has offered me a framework to think from, and to carry this clinical work without running away from it. It's not that I had much self-confidence in working with the woman I've just discussed. But I didn't think to merely psychoeducate and listen to her; I invited her to speak instead. Sure, I was anxious as well. It could have gone completely differently, and then that institution would have thought: "Evi Verbeke? Oof, you shouldn't send anyone to her." Then I could also have thought: "Yeah, who am I?"

DD: It's an anxiety that makes you work instead of recoil. You have a choice in how you deal with that anxiety.

EV: Yes. I think that only succeeds through further clinical formation and dialogue with your supervisor and analyst. I had the realisation that, although I had graduated, I didn't have access to knowing what to do after my training. It is a job I have committed myself to. From there I'm trying to contribute to psychoanalysis myself, and I'm continuing to educate myself. It doesn't stop here.

DD: Yes, working with an analyst, a supervisor, and, as you pointed out, some others as well…

EV: Indeed. I have never limited speaking about my work to my own analyst and supervisor. I have always sought out people to talk with about what happens, what affects me, and how not to bother patients with what affects me. I started doing that back when I was in training by talking to fellow students about psychoanalysis, but I have continued to do so ever since. Psychoanalysis is a practice of speech, but I believe that this speech should also occur outside of the therapeutic situation. It involves speaking in different ways, including from your own perspective as a subject (in analysis), from a clear framework about the patient (in supervision), and through casual, informal conversations with others. Speaking to others about our work, isn't that a necessary prerequisite for what we do?

DD: I completely agree. Thank you for speaking so openly about that work here!

EV: With great pleasure!

Notes

1 Freud, S. (1955 [1920]). *The Psychogenesis of a Case of Homosexuality in a Woman. Standard Edition, XVIII*, 145–174. The Hogarth Press, London
2 Verbeke, E. (2022). *Psychiatrie op Drift: Over Macht, Ethiek en Verzet* [*Psychiatry Adrift: On Power Ethics and Resistance*]. EPO, Berchem.

Chapter 5

Amar El-Omari – The Awakening of a Clinician

Amar El-Omari is currently working on a PhD, where he is studying radicalization and deradicalization (disengagement) within the context of Islam through qualitative research, Lacanian psychoanalysis and literature. Prior to beginning his research, he worked as a psychotherapist in a mental health service in Brussels, where he developed a specific interest in transcultural psychotherapy and the influence of cultural representations and religious beliefs on the way mental suffering and symptoms present themselves in a clinical context. He has written multiple papers on these topics.

Dries Dulsster (DD): I would first like to thank you for wanting to participate in this project. I invited you for a specific reason. A few years back you presented a case study that left an impression on me. You illustrated very nicely how a case can have an impact on your clinical formation, and how this can change the way you position yourself in your clinical practice. Since then, I've noticed how analysts repeatedly refer to the same cases in their presentations or writings. Those are the cases they keep working on, and that seem to have had an impact on them. So, I would love to talk with you about that case. Do you know which one I'm referring to?

Amar El-Omari (AEO): Yes, definitely! I'll call him 'Mohammed', and I'll first somewhat situate this case in time, because my personal context matters to the story. I graduated in 2005, and in 2007 I started working in a centre for mental health care in Brussels. It was a satellite clinic that focused on transcultural and multicultural counselling. The application process for this job was a strange experience, and already the story's first paradox. A few years before, I had said to myself that I would never work in a centre for mental health care, and that I would never work with migrants. Nevertheless, this job I applied for *was* in a centre for mental health care, and they were looking for someone who had expertise in the field of multicultural counselling. I used my ethnic background to get the job, a job that eventually confronted me with myself in the sense that it echoed previous experiences. I had done my internship in *La Borde* clinic, which had been hugely overwhelming. There

DOI: 10.4324/9781003410935-5

were moments when I came close to losing my mind. I then stuffed all of that in a mental box and put it away. My first job after that was at the OCMW (Public Centre for Social Welfare) in Kortrijk as an intercultural mediator, where I had a bit of an overwhelming experience at a party at work. Everyone was being very social, and I felt completely left out. I couldn't connect with anyone, and I failed to participate. I left the party early, and shortly after I called an analyst for the first time, because I didn't know what was going on with me. I went to see him a couple of times, but it felt like a missed encounter. My appointments were planned during the summer months, but he was only able to see me for a few times before going on leave. After his leave, I myself went on a holiday for about a month, and afterwards I just stopped seeing him altogether. And then, many months after that, I started working at this centre for mental health care, but something in me lingered. Something of which I rationally knew was part of me. So, my answer to the question 'Who is your Dora?' is situated in this context entirely. I was only able to grasp what was actually going on with me through my encounter with Mohammed. That's when all of it came to the surface. It took patients like him to notice that something of myself, as a subject, was at play. Something that, before Mohammed, had really stuck by me as well was an encounter with a woman in her 60s of Moroccan origin. She was referred to me by the general practitioner. In this transference, I was enormously confronted with shame. She also addressed me as 'my son,' which paralysed me. Shame is very present within Moroccan culture. There are things you just don't talk about, and I couldn't get past it. I saw this woman only a few times, and she consulted me concerning some psychosomatic complaints. While talking about that, aspects about her marriage started to slowly enter the conversation, like how unhappy she was in her marriage as a woman. She also had a sense of failure as a mother, and aspects of her sexuality appeared in these conversations as well. But I wasn't capable of naming any of it. I couldn't grasp these topics. I couldn't question anything that touched it, because I was immensely paralysed by that shame. As I mentioned, she referred to me as 'my son', and she evoked something maternal in me. I couldn't intervene as a clinician, because she mirrored a mother to me, and I silently answered her 'my son' with a 'yes, mother'. This situation coupled with, how in Islam, gender separation is an imperative, resulted in shame influencing my counter-transference. The transference became cultural rather than analytical. Imaginary, in other words. The treatment ended after a couple of sessions. Encounters with patients like these made me realise that my own baggage was involved, and that I needed to do something about it. Following this experience, I started my own analysis again. Psychoanalysis is a practice of speech, but I also had to act. I had not been to Morocco for seven years, so during the summer when I started working at the centre for mental health care, I went back again for the first time. The following year-and-a-half I went back five or six times – once every three months and twice in the summertime.

Something was pushing me. There was something I needed to know. I was constructing something through speaking with my analyst, but there was also something that had to be created through speaking with others. Very specifically, some family members needed to help me understand parts of my parents' story. It was during the time I went back and forth to Morocco that the encounter with Mohammed took place.

DD: In any case, you immediately illustrate that people can only become 'Dora's' from a specific, personal context. Something of the unconscious is at stake.

AEO: Without a doubt. In meeting Mohammed, I encountered myself – or rather, I was forced to face myself if I wanted to take my clinical work somewhat seriously. I met Mohammed in the fall of 2008, and in this meeting all the missed encounters with other patients, like the woman I just talked about, came together. I realised that I had thought I understood what their problem was. I had sinned against the basic rule of keeping yourself from thinking you know already. By having this idea of 'knowing' them, I did not have to face myself. Mohammed was referred to me by his family doctor with a series of stress-related complaints after an accident at work. She thought it would be a good idea for him to talk to a psychologist. I indicated to him at the beginning that it was absolutely possible if he preferred to speak Arabic or Moroccan. However, he insisted on speaking French. He said: "I am educated, and I am integrated. I'm not one of those migrants who don't know the language." This message was accompanied with a certain anger. So I said French was not a problem either. Initially, he only wanted to come every two weeks. I made a working hypothesis that this remark was part of his obsessional neurosis, with some narcissistic injury – an affront in part related to the injury of being a migrant. I also made this hypothesis, this construct, through academic literature. At the time, I was reading a lot about anything to do with multicultural and transcultural counselling. I felt it was a great hypothesis. I thought of myself as super tough and super smart. I thought I had him completely figured out already after a few sessions. The problem was that he wasn't cooperative. It was a very frustrating experience: "I know what the problem is, I know what needs to be done, but he doesn't cooperate!" I also didn't understand why he never missed an appointment, because I felt he wasn't bringing me anything anyway... At our house they call that 'Buzbuz'.

DD: Buzbuz?

AEO: A kind of disturbance in thinking. Like those omens when you're about to get a migraine, but you're trying to hold it back, even though you know it's futile. It's when something starts to irritate you, and you try to push it away. Analytically I would say that it was where I was hit in my subjectivity, but I refused to let it throw me off balance. I was refusing to give up the response I had awkwardly formulated to 'I'm never going to work in a centre for mental health care.' I didn't want to 'pay with my person' as Lacan states in *The Direction of the Treatment and the Principles of Its Power*.[1] So it felt like he had come to disturb something within me. He was very present in the room, never stayed seated. There were always things that bothered him a little. Either the sunlight was bothersome, and the curtain had to be closed. But instead of asking, he started fumbling the curtain. Or the chair bothered him, because it wasn't comfortable enough. There was always something. He got up a few times, and said there was no point in coming to talk to me, so he wanted to leave. And then he said: "But since I'm here already, I'll talk anyway." He also got angry: "Why are you continuously writing this down?" I then added my own colonial hypothesis, namely that he was one of those people who don't know what therapy is, and that I had to explain it to him. That I took notes to structure my thoughts a bit. I also showed him the notes so he could see that they often were nothing but scribbles. Of course, this was something very imaginary on my behalf: 'You won't touch my way of working.' I stuck to my framework. When the end of the year approached, I left for Morocco again. I was at the airport with only carry-on luggage, which had been checked and caused all my stuff to become jumbled. In order not to dawdle there, I decided to organise my things again at the gate. So, I'm sitting there, rearranging my luggage, and suddenly I hear Mohammed. I was bewildered. He was sitting not that far from me, talking to someone else. I was tremendously startled. I was not in my role as a therapist. I wasn't dressed for it, whatever that means. I was wearing sweatpants, with my stuff all over the place. After feeling bewildered, I became angry. I had seen him the day before, and I was like: "But, you didn't say anything about going to Morocco." I also wondered what he was doing here. It was a very territorial reaction. It was not so much about the fact that he was at the airport, but rather that he was not from the same region in Morocco as me. All these thoughts happened in a matter of seconds. I'm not proud of it, but it was what it was. Then I heard him again, because he had a very loud voice. It was inappropriately loud, because he didn't fit the context. In therapy he was always very loud as well, on the phone, in the waiting room, on the stairs. It was now early in the morning, he was very loud, and I looked up. We looked at each other, but he didn't see me. No, he did *see* me, but he didn't *recognise* me. There was nothing in his eyes. It was a very strange experience for me, and I didn't understand. I then continued to tidy my belongings on the floor, and, again, I see him, I hear him and he passes me by. We look at each other once more, and still I don't see any signs of recognition. But I was happy with it. At that moment, I was not concerned with what it meant or what was going on. I was just relieved to have some anonymity. At the same time, I was revelling in the absurdity of the situation. I started imagining he would be sitting next to me on the plane, that he would ask to get a ride together, etc.

My mind took it very far. Then I heard they were calling for him in all languages: "Mohammed is asked at the gate. Last call." But he didn't respond. At first, I was glad it was a different gate, so we were not going to be on the same plane. He was called again and again, but he didn't respond. I then felt this dilemma: should I do something, should I approach him and say they are calling for him? But then I started to wonder what that would mean. The session the day before had gone badly. He had gotten very angry because of me taking notes. I had told him I was going on leave, and he had asked for an appointment for when I would return. They kept calling his name, and I started negotiating with myself. On the one hand, I thought it wasn't my problem, that I shouldn't care. On the other hand, I thought I couldn't do that. It's like watching an accident that's about to happen, and you're not intervening. Then there was a very small part of me that was thinking professionally: "What is happening here? What is going on? Should I intervene? What will the effect be?" But before I could decide on what to do, I saw him getting up and going to his gate. I was rid of my dilemma, but I then and there called a supervisor to set up an appointment for Mohammed after my vacation.

DD: An immediate decision!

AEO: Yes, afterwards I got to talk about it in supervision, and I thought about it for a while. I was also irrationally angry with him, because now I had occupied myself with work during my leave. It was all very strange. The entire flight I was wondering what had happened. And while I was pondering, all his sessions came back to me – especially pieces of his story that I seemed to have repressed, because they did not fit my hypotheses. Suddenly I could see him as a man with a psychotic structure. For him I only existed as a psychologist, but not outside of that. Regarding the parts of his story I had forgotten about, two elements were important: his relationship to language and fatherhood. Concerning language, my hypothesis connected to that bit of: "Mohammed, you can speak Arabic in here", and his response: "I will speak French. I studied and I am educated." He grew up in Morocco. He had finished high school and wanted to continue studying, but ultimately did not. However, he had always been into literature and reading, and had always been very good at it. About the effect of the accident, he said: "I am losing language. I have been here for several years. I spoke Dutch pretty well, but after the accident, I lost it. I sometimes lose access to Dutch." He also began to make mistakes, and was very sensitive to it. For him, it was unbearable that before the accident he could pronounce everything and formulate correct sentences. His French was no longer 100 per cent there anymore either. 'I am losing language', was a complaint of his. There was also tension in his body, accompanied by a tingling in his fingers. At times, he felt that his fingers were half paralysed. The family doctor had assigned these sensations to stress.

Stress was also present concerning fatherhood. Mohammed was a man in his 30s, married, with two children. He had worked for several years before he suffered the work-related accident, after which he dropped out of work. Then he had to go through a lot of hassle for the accident to be acknowledged as a workplace accident, but it didn't happen. They kicked him off social security benefits, and they hunted him down to go back to work. He didn't understand why he didn't qualify for it to be recognised as a workplace accident, since it had indeed happened with a machine at his workplace. He had also just become a father to a son at the time of the accident. When I questioned certain topics during his preliminary interviews, this issue had also come up. He wanted to be a good Muslim man: to be a good husband, to put bread on the table. Now he only received very limited benefits, and that was hurtful to him. He could no longer provide financially, but being able to provide was important to him in being a father to his son. I had ignored all of that, because it didn't fit the construction I had made. Before, I had read what he had told me in the direction of a depressive reaction following the affront to the ideal image of how he needed himself to be – a vision he could no longer meet. But he wasn't particularly concerned with the Other either. That's why I wanted to situate him towards obsessional neurosis rather than hysteria. But while I was sitting on that plane, a chronology began to appear, and suddenly psychosis presented itself as a possibility. When I talked about all of this afterwards in supervision and in my analysis, I realised that something of myself was at stake there. That I had met my 'Dora' at the airport. What I hadn't wanted to see, was how literal I had to take what he was saying: "I don't know how to be a father", resulting in perplexity: "I lose language." The 'good Muslim man' was a certain imperative that acted as a total identification that held him together, but at the same time this compass could not give direction on how to father a son, because he was on foreign soil and this compass seemed to work only on Islamic soil. The moment he lost his job, he radically fell out of his identification: he was no longer a father nor a husband, and thus no longer a good Muslim man. Until then, fatherhood was an element that I hadn't registered before, because I focused mostly on what being a migrant meant to him. By doing so I gave the 'foreignness' more and more consistency. And being foreign was the same alterity that I was very concerned with at that time myself, both in my analysis and in my travelling back and forth to Morocco. Now, for a long time, I also had a strange relationship toward psychosis. Psychosis was my first experience in the clinic. When I started working at the centre for mental health care, I would more often work with neurosis, with what I considered to be 'normal people', whatever that means. Thanks to him, I had to reconsider all of those things. It made me wake up as a clinician!

DD: This nicely demonstrates the issues that can arise at the level of differential diagnosis. It certainly depends on our theoretical knowledge, but also on the fact that 'the neurotic always knows how to find the neurotic'. This means

that we may completely ignore some elements of a psychotic structure due to our own neurosis. While a supervisor can point this out, it is often a delicate matter. Furthermore, as you have pointed out, there are many biases regarding the diagnosis of psychosis.

AEO: Indeed. In retrospect I recognised how I was seeing Mohammed as a double, and therefore basically treating myself. Mohammed has been so crucial to me, because I was very caught up in diagnostics and my own story. The neurotic indeed finds the neurotic. It was my own search, my own baggage. My thinking was really disturbed. The idea of going to Morocco for a vacation was gone. It was no longer possible not to think about the diagnostic issue concerning Mohammed for the entire flight. I started scribbling and writing, and suddenly another logic appeared. And I felt like such an idiot for not having seen it before. I had also just gone along with the family's doctor's story that Mohammed had epilepsy, and I hadn't considered any other explanation for how he related to his symptoms. As a result, he was given the diagnosis of an acquired brain injury. I hadn't questioned it at any point. But one of the first things he had said to me was: "I'm a father of a son, and I don't know how to be a father of a son in a foreign country." Like I mentioned earlier, he felt it was impossible for him to be a father in a non-Muslim context, and the accident at work made him lose the role of a good Muslim man. That was his issue: "I cannot be a good Muslim man." I could suddenly hear it. I could also reinterpret that experience as hypochondriacal, an elementary phenomenon. Afterwards, I could interpret everything about the accident as a delusion, but one rooted in reality. There was a legal battle going on concerning the accident, but I suddenly realised that it had taken a delirious form. There, too, I had been too focused on the normality of what he said to me. I had asked few questions about how he related to that experience, and how it had been for him, and what was at stake. There was no way to engage in a dialectic process. The entire ordeal was a way for him to recover something. There had been a violation of his idea of 'being a man'. If he could receive recognition concerning the accident, he could also receive recognition as someone who simply wasn't able to work, which then meant that he could still be a man and have some right to exist. A good Muslim man has to work and provide for his family, but if you suffered an accident, not working becomes understandable. Another delirious construction appeared three years later. He said: "My face is not my face anymore. Don't you see the scars?" I saw nothing, and he showed a tiny scar that might as well have been a remnant of chickenpox. Had he not pointed it out to me, I would have never noticed. He felt the plastic surgeon had not done a proper job. He also said that when he got his recognition, he would sue that doctor, and they would have to fix his face. He also talked about this issue with his social worker and psychiatrist, and

I told them not to get into it. I told them: "The more you talk about it, the more consistency you're giving it. So just let it be." Eventually, he got his recognition, which made him financially secure.

DD: I would like to circle back to your comment of "being awakened as a clinician". Being asleep meant being stuck in the idea of a certain therapeutic frame and an idea about diagnostics. It is a good example of the master's discourse: not wanting to be disturbed, not in one's own practice, not in one's own thinking.

AEO: I have to say that, for years, it tied together with how I presented myself. I couldn't present myself as a clinical psychologist, based on the idea that I would otherwise put myself in some kind of master's position. At least, that was what I had deluded myself into thinking. It was supposedly a clever way to make sure I didn't coincide with the master's discourse. But, of course, the master's discourse appeared on an entirely different level anyway: how I thought about multiculturalism, my own framework, my own difficulties. During my internship in *La Borde* clinic, I also didn't really know which position to take in clinical work. I started a psychodynamic training to become a psychotherapist, but then I was given these technical seminars about the payments, the number of sessions, what the exact distance should be between the chairs...

DD: As opposed to the discourse of the master, there's the discourse of the analyst. The latter has no predetermined framework, no predetermined ideas around number of sessions, the cost of the sessions, what one should be talking about, the duration of the sessions. An analyst just has his act, by placing himself in an analytic discourse.

AEO: Mohammed has been a compass for me to find my way back to the Lacanian way of thinking. In my psychodynamic training, during supervision, this was interpreted as narcissism, and I translated it for myself as him being obsessional. In retrospect, that turned out to be beside the point. And so, Mohammed became a compass, not only towards diagnosis, but also concerning how to intervene. He allowed, or maybe even forced, me to stop reading all these books on multiculturalism.

DD: Is it too strong to say that you needed this clinical encounter to push something forward in your own analysis?

AEO: It allowed for a kind of acceleration in my own analysis that I can't put into words. It has influenced me as a clinician and as a human being. It provoked a subjective division in me, and at the same time it made me face that division. I think that's also when I was able to start thinking clinically, or rather, when I could try to think separately from my neurosis surrounding multiculturalism and shame. In any case, since then, I have been able to see a lot faster when something of my own neurosis is getting involved. I am now capable of inhabiting my supervision and my analysis in a different way, and thus of positioning myself differently in clinical practice. I can't put it any other way than that. Now I could be a clinician, I could be present, I could intervene and break free from certain ideas. Even though I had already read about it theoretically, experiencing that there are no rules has been crucial. Psychoanalysis is something you have to reinvent every time, which is a liberating idea. It is important to clinically colour outside the lines when needed, though of course there's an ethical aspect to doing so.

DD: It's about starting to grasp there is no such thing as a colouring book.

AEO: Yes, indeed. I tried too keenly to fit the mould of how I thought I had to be, so I mirrored others, such as my own analyst. But that doesn't work in a centre for mental health care. I couldn't always use what my analyst did. I could only distil that I had to be quiet and do nothing but say: "See you next time!" Suddenly, I understood why I did certain things. I went from 'thinking' to a 'psychoanalytic act'. And perhaps I should add that my diagnostic switch with respect to Mohammed was not without difficulty. It was very threatening to him. Where before I just said 'hm' and interpreted, suddenly everything was possible. I became completely enigmatic. Suddenly my style was completely different. I started talking about it with my supervisor on a weekly basis, because I felt something was at stake. If I'm honest about it, something was at stake for myself concerning my ability to be a clinician: 'Do I want that, can I do that?'

DD: I think that's a phase we all have to go through.

AEO: Gradually, I was able to become a helping other for him. For example, I had ignored that he had brought Koranic verses to the sessions, but after the switch, I let him teach me about the Koran, and we found a therapeutic formula where he came to the sessions to give me Koranic lessons. He thought it was funny that he had to pay for doing that. I was able to let go of the serious tone of the existential themes that were at play. I then emphasised conversation more, and gave less consistency to being a migrant, which also allowed me to take my work more seriously. So, Mohammed was my Dora, because he has allowed me to feel what it truly means to be a clinician. He has allowed me to find my way back to Lacanian psychoanalysis. After obtaining my master's degree in psychology, I had drifted away without realising it – especially concerning the importance of ethics.

DD: An encounter that made you return to Lacanian psychoanalysis and its ethics, that seems like a good note to finish the interview on. I can't thank you enough for speaking so openly about all of this.

AEO: You're welcome.

Note

1 Lacan, J. (2002c [1957]). *The Direction of the Treatment and the Principles of Its Power*. In *Ecrits* (pp. 489–542). [English ed. translated by Bruce Fink]. Norton.

Chapter 6

Annie Rogers – The Unconscious Signs its Letters

Annie Rogers, PhD, professor emerita of psychoanalysis and clinical psychology, is a recipient of a Fulbright Fellowship at Trinity College, Dublin, Ireland; a Radcliffe Fellowship at Harvard University; a Whiting Fellowship at Hampshire College; and an Erikson Scholar at Austen Riggs. She has conducted studies on a range of topics, including girls' psychological development and trajectories of change in child analysis, as well as studies of language and visual art in psychosis. She served as co-director of Hampshire's Psychoanalytic Studies Program. She is the author of *A Shining Affliction: A Story of Harm and Healing in Psychotherapy* (1996), *The Unsayable: The Hidden Language of Trauma* (2007) and *Incandescent Alphabets: Psychosis and the Enigma of Language* (2018). Currently she is a supervising analyst and vice-president at the Lacanian School of San Francisco, and an associate member of the Association for Psychoanalysis and Psychotherapy in Ireland.

Dries Dulsster (DD): So, Annie, first of all I want to thank you for participating in this project. Now, when I asked you the question "Who is your Dora?", you immediately replied:

Annie Rogers (AR): "What if there is more than one?" (*laughs*)

DD: Indeed. I think it would be strange if there was only one! So, where do you want to start?

AR: I've already written about some of this,[1] but what comes to mind immediately is that in my doctoral internship – I was already interested in psychoanalysis as a teenager – I sought out a site where I could work with children and my supervisor could be a psychoanalyst. There was one particular little boy whom I called Ben in the book – that is not his real name – who had a profound effect on the way I looked at and thought about the unconscious. I followed him in his play and speech. The milieu of the treatment centre, which was a residential one, was not psychoanalytic itself. People were more interested in behavioural changes and setting goals for the

DOI: 10.4324/9781003410935-6

children. Not that those things are unimportant, because, for children who are very disturbed, they *are* pretty important. But this little boy really, really, required space to play and speak. What emerged was extraordinary. It was an unfolding of a trauma that he could not possibly have remembered. It was way too early in his life, and it came directly into his play. He also gradually realised that he was able to make use of the play therapy space and his time with me to do and say things, and to behave in a way he couldn't anywhere else. At the time he was 5 years old and living with a foster family who wanted to adopt him. He slept in what is called a bubble bed: a bed that is like a crib, but enclosed, so he wouldn't be able to get out at night and hurt himself. He sometimes ran out in front of cars, and in the classroom he had to be restrained several times every day because he would explode into rages. It happened *once* in the entire nine months that I worked with him. Anyway, more than anything he showed me the power of the unconscious. His trauma was not in his records, but one day we were playing outside, and he played out the scene of a fire in which he assigned the roles and all the dialogue. I had the sense that there was something, in Lacan's terms, very real about this. And the one time he had lost it completely with me, I also realised that it was screaming rage. It wasn't rage about a thing, it was way beyond that. So, I started looking into his records, and eventually I found someone who was willing to give me – a young intern in her 20s – information that had been left out of all his files, which is that as a baby he had been born to a mother who didn't want him and who wasn't able to raise a child. He ended up in a first foster family, who left him in a dark room alone for much of the time he was with them. Social services discovered this child when a fire broke out in the house. He had been left behind. I was astonished when I discovered this. It made me more than ever trust the process and that he would lead me in. I came to understand his play as a form of dreamwork with the unconscious, and I simply followed him. That was the first case. Very, very powerful.

DD: So, you say it shifted how you thought about the unconscious? Do you remember how you thought about it before and after?

AR: Before I had read Freud, I had read the object relation theorists. I didn't know that in a child, or in a child so young that there had been no memory, something could have left a trace so strong that he would need to play it out. Not only the way that he played it out was important, but he also gave it a new ending.

DD: He gave it a new ending during the session where he played it out?

AR: Yes. In the fire scene he was playing, it was the mother who was left and burned in the house, not the child. He assigned me the role of the witness, and he was able to get the baby out and hand it to me. Somehow there was some trace of this old experience that survived in him, and it spoke to me as a young intern. I knew there was something bigger at stake for him. He and his mother had a difficult pregnancy, he had had one foster family, and then another. He had initially been diagnosed as autistic. He seemed *that* out of touch with the world. But there was no way this child was autistic. He was too eloquent in his play and speech. However, this didn't become evident until he had a space to play. So yes, this experience had a profound impact on me. All I had before was theory. (*laughs*)

DD: Was there also tension between theory and clinical practice?

AR: There was a difference. I worked with a child analyst in my supervision. She asked me what I thought. I had read quite a bit of theory by then, and she did not ask for more. Theory was left in the background most of the time.

DD: You said it made you trust the process of what the child was doing, what he was saying?

AR: Yes, yes. This child was my guide.

DD: So, after he played that out, it changed the clinical picture? He played out that scene and...

AR: No, it was more gradual than that. In a very real sense, I didn't know what I was doing, so I followed him completely. I remember the very first session; I sat down and I waited for him to begin, and he played out a scene where he turned out the light in the playroom. He then said: "Don't leave me in the dark." And again, I remember that line coming from him during our first meeting and thinking, there's something here...

DD: There is something here.

AR: Yes, it was about this 'something' I could not quite grasp or name, which gradually unfolded over that year.

DD: I must say that I'm very curious about that one time in those nine months that he exploded. What happened?

AR: He had made a set of papier mâché wings to be in a Christmas play. He brought them into the playroom to show me. He was 5 years old; he was clumsy. He put his arm in on one side and then he put his other arm straight through the other wing. Not the armhole. He completely lost it. Any 5 or 6 year old would be falling apart after having worked on such a project and then destroying their wings – I get that. But there was something in his breathing, his crying, his pounding his head against the floor of which I thought: this is something much bigger. This is just a form for it.

DD: "There's something there", and you said you have written about this. That is also something that struck me in the previous interviews: analysts seem to write about these cases. So, how was that for you?

AR: It was a very important case for me. There was also something there from my side, from my experience. I was seven months into my doctoral, clinical internship when I had an acute psychotic break. By 'acute' I don't mean for a couple of days, but for three months. So, it took me away from him for a while.

DD: That was during his treatment?

AR: That was during the year I was working with him. Another very powerful realisation I had upon returning from that experience, and from continuing to work with him, was that I became convinced he would not be able to continue the work. I expected that he would have sealed himself off completely. But that was not the case. I was shocked. I think there was something about the loss and the return that again allowed him to work through something of the level of the real. My own analysis was unfolding alongside this treatment, and I realised that there was nothing in print – that I knew of – that laid out, side by side, an analytic experience by a clinician in an encounter with a patient. Or something that touched on the changes in play therapy alongside the changes in the early months of my own analysis. For me, it seems like she is looking in that book for herself.

DD: That is probably the best reason to write a book. It also seems that it can sometimes even be a blessing to take a break from our clinical work for some time.

AR: I have found that to be true. It is vital to take breaks, to allow analysands space to go on and just live and see what has remained the same and what has changed. But in the case of this child, the break was a huge risk, and not one I'd chosen.

DD: Something else that strikes me about this case is that the boy was diagnosed with autism. However, you noticed through the eloquence of his play that this was not the case. There was a difference between the image in the institution and in the playroom. Could you elaborate on that?

AR: It was one of the more mystifying things about this child for me. I understand where the diagnosis came from. He hated being touched by his second set of foster parents who were extraordinarily good to him and incredibly patient. He also exploded repeatedly in the classroom. There were times where he did all kinds of dangerous things. He had to sleep in this confined space, because he could not be trusted. You know, when he came into the playroom, I simply followed him. I had no idea what I was doing, but by following him, he set the pace. He created the play. He used the paint. He took us outdoors. He took us indoors. He made costumes. He told me my part to play. From the beginning, he was like a different child in that space.

DD: Creating a space for a child, without knowing what to do, seems to have important effects. The institution thought it knew what it was doing, so there was no space for the child.

AR: What you have said is eloquently put.

DD: When I talked to Stijn Vanheule about the patient that influenced him, he learned that it was not about the master's discourse, but the analyst's discourse. When he started to let go of mastering it all, other things became possible. That is also what you kind of pinpoint in this case: 'I didn't know what I was doing, and therefore things could change in a certain way.' It's 'not knowing what to do', starting from a certain theory, but nonetheless...

AR: Yes, nonetheless, without knowing how to name what I was doing, I inhabited what Lacan calls 'the lack', that space of listening which creates effects in the unconscious.

DD: It's remarkable that it comes up again. I don't know if you would like to add something about Ben?

AR: I might come back to him, because there was a second major experience that comes to mind. By the late 1990s, I had finished my doctoral degree and I had gone to Harvard as a research associate. I did a post-doctoral internship at the Erikson Centre in Cambridge, Massachusetts, and I was appointed to the Harvard Faculty. During those early years, I started a very small private practice – usually two children, that was it. As an academic I'm sure you can appreciate that it was a very full-time position. I was working with Harvard faculty member and researcher Carol Gilligan in the late 1980s, early 1990s, around the psychological development of girls. While I was involved in that research and published about it, people started to refer adolescent girls to me. There was a girl who I met when she was 11. I have also written about her and there I called her Ellen.[2] I was absolutely compelled to write. She did not want to come and see me. However, her parents did come to see me, because they had recently learned that she had suffered sexual abuse when she was 5 or 6 years old. She had never spoken about it. I had not gone to a patient's home before, but in this singular instance, I did. I went to their home. So, I had broken the usual frame or boundary of meeting in an office only. I said: "Give her a chance to look me over, so she can see what I am like." I had dinner with them. She had a little brother. They had a large Labrador. We sat, we talked, we had coffee. They tried to get her to speak, but I said that she didn't need to do anything. After that meeting, with no pressure on her whatsoever, she said that she wanted to come and see me.

DD: Going to someone's home is not something a lot of analysts would do, I think, but it seemed to have been important.

AR: Yes, I believe there are times that require a singular act as an invitation to a subject. You cannot force speech, but you can invite a child as a choosing subject. So, she came to see me in my playroom space at Harvard, and... I can't remember if it was the first or second session, but it was really early in the treatment. I had said the name of the boy who had abused her – I used a pseudonym in my writing and also here. In fact, I had to completely rewrite the case to change all the names. She came in and she put her head in her hands, and said: "My head hurts." And I just said back to her: "Ed hurts." She then flung herself out of the chair, and ran out of the room. I can tell you, an 11 year old runs very fast. She ran out into the traffic, and left her mother and me behind – her mother had been in the waiting room. I thought: "Holy shit... what just happened?" And I said to the mother: "Go home and wait for her." She did just that. The girl made her way on the subway, and she came home. The parents called me that evening. I checked in and I said that I wanted to see her tomorrow. Not next week, tomorrow. And so, she came back, and she asked me: "What was that?" She knew something big had happened. And I said: "I can't tell you what that was. You tell me." She then described how she had heard something that was frightening to her. She had then run outside, and at some point, in making her way home, she had peed herself. It took her into a space of remembering this older boy peeing on her. That was how she had interpreted the ejaculation, and we were suddenly in the midst of that scene. I knew something about how to work with trauma, and I had also worked with Bessel van der Kolk and his group – at the time he was at the forefront of how the body reacts to and how it stores trauma. But I was also really intrigued with Lacan. I had stumbled upon the *Ecrits* in a bookstore, and I read it and thought it was brilliant. I couldn't read it, but it's brilliant...

DD: Yes, I recollect that moment for myself as well. Sitting on the train, happy that I'd finally bought a copy, starting to read and then having the experience I had no idea what was going on...

AR: In order to learn how to read it, I joined a Lacan reading group and met a Lacanian analyst and others who were living in Cambridge. That unfolded side by side the early years of this case and these encounters. I found myself listening – as I had with the younger children – to the play and looking at the drawings as if they were dreams unfolding in front of me, but also being able to listen for signifiers and particular potential connections among them and the work that unfolded over time. I worked with 'Ellen' for seven years, and as it unfolded it led her to a transgenerational trauma. This was why it was so impossible for her to speak to her parents about what had happened to her. There was a story of a great-aunt who had been an adolescent in the Holocaust, and who had been captured by the Nazis. She didn't know of the existence of this aunt. The aunt had been promiscuous as a teenager, and the idea of talking about sexuality in that household was unthinkable. Over the seven years we worked together, Ellen changed immensely. Though between age 11 and age 17, you'd change extraordinarily anyway. She started to play the cello, and she got accepted into a very prestigious music school. But what struck me the most was, again, the replication of my earlier clinical experience – if you follow the threads of the play and take it seriously, as if you're hearing a dream unfold, the child will lead you exactly to where they need you to go. But then I also had the capacity to begin to think about the unconscious through signifiers, and I noticed for instance that when she came for a while, and she wanted to talk about her friends at school and what was going on and how she negotiated her way through tensions and remarks that she found offensive, I followed that intensely and I lost track of listening to the unconscious through signifiers.

DD: It's the times we let ourselves be bamboozled by the imaginary ego of the subject and lose track of the symbolic signifiers.

AR: Indeed, and then things just went dead. She was an adolescent girl, terrified of what she was living and afraid to speak about it. But when I shifted to the level of dreams, to the level of signifiers in her speech, something else happened. It provoked her and it provoked the unconscious. I could see this in action. It made a change in the way I was working with children and adolescents.

DD: When you said: "Ed hurts", and the immense effect this had on Ellen… It made me think about a remark a student gave me some weeks ago: "I'm scared to intervene." But you just went for it.

AR: I encounter that too in supervision cases. People can be extremely wary of acting or of saying something. I think in part it comes from my own experience, from my own analysis. I did two analyses. In my first analysis I met with an extraordinarily gifted analyst who didn't dance around things. Whatever there was in the room or in my speech, he went right for it. That had already emerged in my earlier work when I was still working with young children aged 5, 6, 7. For years it persisted. But then I joined the Lacanian reading group, which overlapped with the seven years of this case, and I also took seminars offered by the Freudian School of Quebec in Canada. All of this, again, gave me a real sense of the power of this kind of work. They talked about working with adults on the couch. My work with the adolescent girl was not that, but enough of it transferred to be really, really useful to me, and it was at that point where I knew that this would be the direction my life and work would take.

DD: These interviews are about the effect patients have, but you also stress the importance of analysis and the reading groups. It's like there's an interplay between all those things that make the work possible.

AR: Yes, absolutely! It is the interplay between all those facets. I would say that analysis is the ground. There was the way in which... well, let me back-track. By the time I was 13 – and definitely by the time I was 16, 17 years old – I was in psychosis. I was going from one hospitalisation to the next. In the early years of that, my most profound experience was that people could not bear to listen to me speaking about anything that mattered to me, or anything that was real and that I was experiencing. They did not want to hear it. They wanted to medicate me, send me back to school, and let me get on with life. And I did that on the one hand, but on the other hand, I fell into a crisis every few months. I had this profound sense that people were frightened of my experience. In meeting that little boy and realising from the beginning there was something at stake beyond something in his record that I could not understand, I was devoted to find out what that was. I did not have any theory to accompany me, other than having read Freud. A little Guntrip, a little Melanie Klein, a little bit of this and that. I just didn't know. But that was already at work in me. After this psychotic break when I was in graduate school, I met my first analyst, and that analysis changed my life. It allowed me to enter lucidity as a ground to walk on and to sustain. That was some-thing I had never experienced before. This unfolded alongside my work with Ben, and it enabled me to finish my degree, go to Harvard, work with Gilli-gan, apply, get the job to work on the faculty and meet Ellen – the 11-year-old girl – and it was only then that I discovered Lacan.

DD: And so you were 'compelled' to write about it. Could you tell me more about that? What is that about?

AR: Before I turned to my clinical training, I wrote. I wrote and I drew. It was just part of who I was. When I realised that there was no book in the clinical world that addressed what I wanted to say about my work, I decided to write that book myself. This work, interrupted by a psychotic crisis, was then connected to my own analysis that had changed my life. I wrote about it to speak to a field that didn't yet have that in it. And then with the Ellen case, I had the same kind of impulse. I hadn't thought about it before this interview. The Lacanian world has a lot of vignettes, but not a lot of detailed clinical cases. This is for many good reasons. But in the early 2000s, mid-2000s, people in the American clinical field had no knowledge of Lacan. They thought I was mad for following Lacan on this track. But there was something about working with this girl that made me think: I want this to live in the world, I want my field to know about this. When I finished writing the book, I had no idea if I would be able to publish it. So, I met with the girl and gave her the whole manuscript. We talked about the level of disguise in it, and I asked her if she wanted to show it to her parents. She said yes. Meanwhile I was waiting for about a week – I can't remember for how long exactly, it seemed interminable to me. Because the question was: are you alright with me publishing this or not? It was her choice. And yes, she and her parents really wanted me to publish it.

DD: The signifier 'compelled' really strikes me. Obviously, there was a case that had a profound impact on me as well, and on how I thought about psychoanalysis and clinical work. It was the first paper I ever published. I still carry that case with me… It's also like there is something that we need to get out of our system, that we have to try out and understand, or that we think that can be instructive to others.

AR: Yeah, and that brings me to the third case, because I have the feeling that I would want to publish something about him. Because of confidentiality I can't go into much of the details. This is a middle-aged man who I had treated for quite a while. At the very beginning of the treatment, I had the sense he was mystified by his symptom, that it persisted beyond his control, and he suffered from it. There was something illegal involved, and he could not control it. I could see that clearly. At first, he said he was just intellectually interested in Lacanian analysis, and wanted to see what it was all about. I asked him for dreams, and he worked on his dreams. I had less experience with adults on the couch. I had a career with children and adolescents. I didn't have the experience of seeing someone struggle with a symptom that was making his life miserable over a long period of time. He could not stop himself from stealing, mostly little things he did not need and sometimes did not even want, but sometimes things that were very valuable. It took a long time for him to see that there was a pattern and a logic that involved an unconscious address to an Other. This pattern crossed generations and began before my analysand was alive. It had to do with life and death. Towards the end of the analysis, seeing the transformation of that symptom into a new job he had started on – and the kind of joy and wordplay that had become possible late in his analysis – I would have never, ever guessed it would have been possible for this man to change his symptom. It was the first time I really saw the end of an analysis, and what it could look like in neurosis. It was very, very powerful to me, because one of the things that had been daunting for both of us was that a part of his symptom (the jouissance of the address) had been hidden and intractable. But he had made new moves concerning the address, which was extraordinary to witness. The worst of his symptom fell away. These were ethical moves. There is no other word for it, and if I were to write another case, I would want to write about this one.

DD: So, the first encounter seemed to be the unconscious, the second encounter the signifier, and the third encounter jouissance?

AR: Yes, I totally agree with those three. Not that they are evenly divided, but in terms of the unfolding of the work, it's very real.

DD: Is there anything else you'd like to add?

AR: No, nothing else comes to mind. Those are my three!

DD: Well, thanks a lot for your time and willingness to participate.

AR: No problem.

Notes

1 Rogers, A. (1995). *A Shining Affliction: A Story of Harm and Healing in Psychotherapy*. Viking Penguin, New York.
2 Rogers, A. (2006). *The Unsayable: The Hidden Language of Trauma*. Ballantine Books, New York.

Chapter 7

Stephanie Swales – Untrodden Grounds

Stephanie Swales, PhD, is an associate professor of psychology at the University of Dallas, a practising psychoanalyst, a licensed clinical psychologist and a clinical supervisor. She has authored numerous articles and book chapters, as well as two books: *Psychoanalysing Ambivalence with Freud and Lacan: On and Off the Couch* (Routledge, 2019), co-authored with Carol Owen; and *Perversion: A Lacanian Psychoanalytic Approach to the Subject* (Routledge, 2012). She serves as an editor for the PCSreview section of *Psychoanalysis, Culture & Society*, member-at-large for the Association for Psychoanalysis, Culture & Society, as well as for the Dallas Society for Psychoanalytic Psychology, and secretary for the Society for Theoretical and Philosophical Psychology (APA's Division 24).

Dries Dulsster (DD): Hi, Stephanie. Thanks for participating in my Dora-project! Every interview starts with the same question: "Who is your Dora?" What comes to mind? Does this question provoke anything?

Stephanie Swales (SS): Absolutely! It provokes the idea that we are shaped by our patients and analysands, just like we hold an important position in their analytic work. It is fundamental to psychoanalysis. It is an invention of Freud. The first set of people that come to mind are from when I was a graduate student trainee. I was working part-time at an outpatient forensic clinic, where most of the patients were either convicted or prejudicated sexual offenders. It was a practicum training placement that I chose, among other options. I ended up working there for maybe two-and-a-half years, because I really enjoyed the work. An outgoing colleague – who was also in the graduate programme – was transferring me her patient that she had worked with during the year that she had been at the clinic. She had been one of the co-leaders for this patient's open-ended group therapy for sexual offenders. This man had not committed a crime, which was a bit unusual. My colleague had also been his individual therapist, but I was only going to be his individual therapist, not also his group therapist. Her passing comment to me about this analysand was: "You'll love working with him because he is very good at free

DOI: 10.4324/9781003410935-7

association." She knew I was analytically oriented, and I thought that was a good thing. I walked somewhat naively into the second or third session, when he – I don't remember his exact words – not so indirectly threatened to sexually assault me. He said something like: "I could if I wanted to, given how we are seated in this room. I am closest to the door, and there are no windows." I immediately thought: "Oh... I don't think this is a typical obsessional neurotic!" Like, okay, he is not just good at free association. This was relatively early in my graduate studies, but I had already read Lacan. I had also read Bruce Fink's clinical introduction into psychoanalysis, since he was my supervisor at the time. So, I had a lot of help in testing out my new hypothesis that this was not a neurotic obsessional, but a perversely structured individual. Luckily it was possible to resituate my position in a way that ended up being more or less productive, but it was always difficult work. I continued to work with him for the two-and-a-half years that I was there, though it was never as difficult as it was during that second session. Once I had a kind of working formulation of what was going on, I was able to intervene in a different way.

DD: The working formulation being?

SS: By working formulation, I mean initially hypothesising that he was sadistically structured, which stood in contrast to my initial formulation that he was an obsessional whose desire had been hystericised such that he had become curious about his unconscious by virtue of my colleague's comment that he was good at free association – and in fact, my colleague presumably hadn't meant 'free association' so much as she had meant 'the fundamental rule of psychoanalysis to say whatever comes to mind'. I had, furthermore, been hypothesising that his structure was obsessional on account of thinking that perhaps obsessional guilt was behind his decision to seek sex offender treatment, even though he had not committed a related crime. Instead, he was attempting to make his therapist, in the role of the Other, anxious through him unknowingly playing the role of the object *a*. On account of the split in his subjectivity, he was seeking treatment at a forensic practice both to help prop up the authority of the law and to make it his plaything. That was the start of my thinking that all – even though he was not technically a sexual offender – sex offenders, depending on their structural diagnosis, require different approaches to treatment. I knew that going in, but I started to really see that the treatment paradigm in the United States and in Canada – and I'm sure also in other places – was oriented as though it was an addiction. It's the idea of a relapse prevention hybrid with CBT, a one-size-fits-all approach. Beyond that, it was much more geared towards neurotics, and the treatment success was just abysmal and very mixed. This was what inspired my first book on perversion.[1] I also did analytic therapy with other perversely structured analysands – including an exhibitionist who was the subject of one of the chapters of my book. Most of the patients I had there were neurotically structured, which for me was an opportunity to deepen the already inextricably intertwined nature of theory and practice. I really benefited as a clinician from that process.

DD: You present the idea that it's not because someone does 'perverse things' that the case concerns a clinical perversion. It could also be that someone is neurotically or psychotically structured.

SS: Right. Of course, in my book on perversion I elaborate a lot more on differential diagnosis, including considerations of behaviours that might societally be labelled as 'perverse', and the notion of perverse traits versus a perverse structure, etc.

DD: Do you have any idea why he never provoked your co-worker?

SS: Well, we only had his consent for her to share her impressions of him prior to my first session with him, so I couldn't speak with her further because of confidentiality reasons. She really didn't give me much more than that. I learned from the patient that her approach was a more humanistic one, and she did things like smile and say: "I'm glad you're here." She would laugh and sometimes share that she felt uncomfortable with some of his associations. In other words, she was more open to self-disclosure, and I think he played with her in a different way. She did share with me that at times it was unsettling, but she assumed that I would be able to handle it better with an analytic stance. I suppose it wasn't a complete surprise, because of course I was aware of the nature of why he was there and the presenting problem.

DD: How did you respond when he said those things? Do you remember?

SS: I honestly don't remember specifically. It's been so long ago. I don't even remember if I wrote it in the book, though I know I mentioned him briefly. I remember responding with a lot of silence. I do remember ending that session early. I was already practising scansion, but more in a moment of silence charged with tension. I was honestly thinking: "I need to regroup!" I needed to start from a different wavelength. It also became clear that the longer I stayed in that situation, the more he was getting off on it. Actually, I wasn't afraid for my safety. There were people on the other side of the door, you know. But I don't remember if I had a verbal response.

DD: Talking about the 'Dora-cases', I think that for a lot of us these are the cases where we think: "I need to regroup." It happens. The question is how to continue after that. How did you handle that transference?

SS: Something that I left out in my response to your last query, was that I think my analytic abstinence and neutrality were really what helped us out of that enactment. In terms of analytic abstinence, I kept myself out of his treatment as far as possible – that is, I tried to embody the desire of the analyst for the analysis to continue. This way of taking up the role of the analyst helps to limit any personal thoughts or reactions that might arise and potentially be revealed to the patient. But, of course, our own thoughts and feelings inevitably emerge from time to time, and perversely structured analysands can be especially adept at bringing them to the surface. The analysand commented later that he had hoped I would have displayed more of an anxious response than I did. Which is to say that although I tried my best to seem unmoved, I certainly let some of my anxiety be seen. During the first session he had talked about how he sometimes got hugs from his previous therapist. She always greeted him with a smile and a "can't you smile for me?" sort of thing, so I think that was a challenge. I continued to practise abstinence as well as analytic neutrality by maintaining the frame of the analysis and not giving into his demands, including his demand for me to tell him what I thought he should or shouldn't do. I didn't start smiling at the guy, but instead I said: "If you continue to threaten me in this way, I'll just end the session and potentially end the work altogether. And then you can work with someone else." I had to enact a certain limit in order for the analytic work to continue. I said that I work a bit differently than his previous therapist, and that it's up to him to start the sessions and say whatever comes to mind in relation to why he is there. He took this invitation to associate freely in a sense of: 'Oh boy! Am I going to associate freely!' You know, he still referred to it, and that was totally okay. His 'I really feel the urge to get under your skin right now, and make you afraid.' It's a question of what was going on there for him to have that urge at that moment. And so, bit by bit, I had to insert some limits at the beginning, and, bit by bit, I was able to actually make him curious about his own unconscious and his ways of getting off and how this may involve more suffering than he had thought. Another thing that actually helped, was to ask him to sit with his back to me, in order to get the work out of the imaginary as quickly as possible. In working with neurotics, I wouldn't typically introduce the element of the couch until their desire to do the work of analysis had already been initiated, but in this perversely structured patient's case it helped him enter the analytic work. I would add, however, that this seating situation didn't stop him from turning around from time to time to try and read my facial expressions!

DD: You introduced a certain suffering.

SS: Yes. A certain kind of subjective lack in him, and pretty quickly after those initial sessions at that. It worked out. Even though he was maintaining a certain satisfaction via his symptoms, he was, at the same time, dissatisfied with many aspects of his work, love, home and social life, and in speaking about these complaints, analysing his dreams, and so on, he began to be curious about his unconscious and about his contributions to his complaints. Dreams are great in this regard, because they can function as a signifier that introduces doubt. They do so not only regarding the nature of the patient as a speaking being with desire, but also – even to some extent for the pervert – regarding the patient's jouissance.

DD: So, although your co-worker said this man was good at free association, it was preventing him from associating freely that has been key here, in such a way that he could no longer try to get under your skin.

SS: Absolutely. A limit had to be set in order for the analytic work to continue. What followed was a modification to the fundamental rule of psychoanalysis. It was inevitable, of course, that he would continue to try to make me anxious at times, as that was part of his structure. Sometimes this would involve trying to skirt the boundary of the limit I had set up, but to my recollection this didn't involve any additional limit-setting and could be discussed in terms of the transference, and brought back to the level of his desire – to a question about himself – instead of being stuck in the imaginary and the provocation of jouissance.

DD: You also mentioned that you published a book about perversion. Annie Rogers indicated she was 'compelled' to write about those cases, and others seem to have written about the cases they discussed as well. Was that the same for you?

SS: That is fascinating to hear. For me, I always enjoyed case formulation. Just the process, taking process notes after sessions, and frequent supervisory sessions to chat about cases, and then to write... I believe I wrote about that analysand in a formulation class with Bruce Fink, and it ended up being a much longer paper than was required. The process of sitting down and thinking and writing about theory, and how theory illuminates certain things or keeps dark spots about the actual clinical work creates further questions, further ideas and hypotheses. It shows us where we may have gone wrong. I feel like I always gravitated towards this process. This also wasn't my first case formulation that I had written about, but I was inspired to do so. And then the subject of my doctoral dissertation was an earlier version of my book as well, so I wanted to think about different cases, and to think more thoroughly about perverse structure.

DD: The idea of being 'compelled' struck me as well. It made me think about Freud and Breuer and how Breuer encountered Anna O. and how he backed down. Freud encountered something as well, but he wrote about it and

continued his work. The same is true for his Dora case. There seems to be a choice there.

SS: I certainly took it up. It really showed me that my role as analyst in each individual case is to think creatively. Clinical work is about enjoying creativity. I was recently talking to Annie Rogers about this, and we discussed Lacan's notion that to do psychoanalytic work, the patient must be able to play and the therapist has to be engaging. For me it means playing with what's spoken, the signifiers, how you are addressed, what is said and how it is said. I have to think about what is going on with that person, and how I can position myself. How I can listen, what I can say to further the whole work. It felt like relatively untrodden ground. I think I was really interested in wanting to have a better sense of all of this.

DD: It's about wanting to know!

SS: Yes, a desire to know.

DD: You started by saying there was a first set of people... this implies there is also a second set. What other patients come to mind?

SS: Working with groups and couples. From a Lacanian perspective, again, these are relatively untrodden grounds. I had an experience co-facilitating a dialectic behavioural therapy group for women with very severe DSM mood disorders. It was an outpatient group, three hours at a time, three times a week. My then co-therapist was the main therapist, and it was her job to do dialectical behavioural therapy. Somehow, I finagle my way into convincing her to change it up a bit, and to let me do the homework review part, to become more attuned to the actual dynamics of that person and to really focus on them.

DD: You have to be creative to introduce psychoanalysis in the workplace!

SS: Yes, of course! Obviously, we didn't have the time to focus on everybody one by one, but we ended up stretching it out to the first hour and forty-five minutes so that we had more time, and eventually we took over the DBT agenda. I was the worst DBT group therapist ever, so I was lucky enough to have a supervisor who had some training in psychoanalytic theory, and who gave me a ton of leeway in how I worked with patients individually and in groups. In any case, at the time I still hadn't had any formation on group therapy. There were no classes on group therapy. My initial training was readings on the side and supervision, and I followed two long-term groups for sex offenders – most of whom were not mandated to have treatment anymore, so they came voluntarily. That experience then continued in other contexts with my own psychoanalytic groups, and then later my own practice. But right from that point I was thinking: how can I be a Lacanian in a group context? I think my earliest publications were about group work. Please don't read them! It was too early. But I enjoyed the challenge of figuring out what we can take from Lacanian theory in group therapy. I wanted to see how I could shape this to be something of what I feel helped to engage in good work. This continued with doing couples work.

DD: Does a specific couple come to mind? Did they teach you how to work in a Lacanian way with couples?

SS: Well, yes. I was already working with couples pretty early in my clinical work. There is this one couple, a heterosexual couple, that were engaged to be married. They had been together for about a year-and-a-half, and very shortly after they met, the woman had become pregnant. It wasn't planned, but they both wanted the baby. We could say that it was unconsciously planned in terms of not having taken any precautions. The woman in particular felt like she couldn't believe her luck that she had been able to get in a relationship with a man who was very charismatic, very handsome, and had a steady job. She had always thought of herself as an ugly duckling. She was self-conscious about her weight, etc. And then they had a traumatic pregnancy loss at seven months that really unravelled the way in which the two of them fit together, their ways of desiring and enjoying each other. After maybe a month, I started to have an inkling that the man was psychotically structured, although he had never had a psychotic break – again, going to structural diagnosis. There are different ways in relating to mourning, and that was the presenting problem. The way they related to their mourning helped illuminate something of their different structures. The man was, in fact, a melancholic. He existed in two entirely different psychical spaces at the same time: one that was with others in the social world, and another existence characterised by a profound aloneness. There's a lot more to say on differential diagnosis, of course. A great book on the topics of mourning, melancholia and depression that I would like to refer to is *Lacan on Depression and Melancholia*[2] edited by Derek Hood and Stijn Vanheule. The woman was a hysterical neurotic, and, unfortunately – this was early in my clinical work – I was not able to intervene in such a way that the man was able to speak rather than act out... I don't even know; I don't remember the specifics well enough anymore. At some point, the man had a really violent outburst. He felt like she was pushing, pushing, pushing on something that wasn't there in him. He destroyed their apartment, threw things at her, and then he disappeared. She didn't know where he was, so she told me what had happened and that they were broken up. This was maybe five months into their treatment, and I did have the opportunity to continue to work with them, but it shows the trickiness of working with two people.

DD: The trickiness?

SS: Yes, the trickiness of working with two people with different structures. The ways of thinking about what works and what doesn't work in their relationship. Their complaints about their non-rapport with the sexual relationship, how they navigated, how they didn't navigate. I started thinking more deeply about how to position oneself, especially if I'm dealing with a psychotic structure and a neurotic structure simultaneously. The same is true for groups. You don't want to provoke a psychotic break in one person, but on the other hand you want to help another person to explore their unconscious. There's a spectrum of who is present in the room, and it's challenging to work with that.

DD: My reflex is always to split them up, so they each can start their own process. I also think it's hard to speak freely when someone else is in the room.

SS: Yes, it is hard to speak as freely when someone other than the analyst is in the room. With groups, I think it's important to avoid having psychotically structured individuals in a group otherwise comprised of neurotics. With couples, I prefer to take turns having individual sessions in between each couple session – with the individual sessions being a part of the couples' work. This isn't always possible, of course, but for the most part couples with whom I have worked have had at least a few individual sessions in tandem with their couple sessions. By and large, I do find that what Lacan has taught us about how to listen to the analysand's speech works very well, even in couple therapy – a situation with obvious limits to the fundamental rule of psychoanalysis – to move both individuals forward in their analytic work. An analysand's speech has a way of communicating what they don't want to communicate anyway! And when there's a couple comprised of a neurotic and a psychotic, I make couple-as-a-whole interventions as if both partners were psychotic. So, more recently in working with couples, I find that it is especially important, sooner rather than later, to get them to talk about what goes on in the bedroom, their masturbation fantasies, their pornography habits, etc. It's not like I have a certain set of questions, but I feel it's needed whenever there is a conspicuous absence of the mention of sex or the details. I feel as though in my earlier work, I may have waited for too long to bring up the absence. So much can be revealed about the crux of their different positions vis-à-vis the object and the other, their repetition compulsion etc., about their jouissance in and out of the bedroom.

DD: Could you maybe illustrate this?

SS: I'm thinking, for instance, of one heterosexual cis-gendered couple, with the man being an obsessional and the woman being a hysteric. They requested to work with me because it was the woman's condition for getting back together with her boyfriend, whom she had been with for a year-and-a-half. The man, I'll call him Jorgé, had recently undergone what had been another, though more indirectly posed, condition: a 'penile enhancement surgery', as the woman – I'll call her Sheila – had complained bitterly and relentlessly about Jorgé's 'skinny dick' and had, without Jorgé asking her to do so, presented him with detailed research on penile enhancement surgery and possible surgeons. It soon became apparent that Sheila's primary object was the phallus, and that she desired a man like her own father, but one who was even more the epitome of uncastrated masculinity. She wanted a big dick in all senses of the term. Her dream man not only had a big penis, but would also be powerful, powerfully built, handsome, intelligent, with an important job, rich, etc., and in her dreams such a man also acted like a dick. At the same time, she, being a hysteric, identified with the role of such a man, and with Jorgé, and she was in many ways a kind of modern-era femme fatale. He had the looks, confidence, intelligence, a penchant for doing and selling illegal drugs, driving recklessly, and so on. Except for his skinny dick, Jorgé had initially fit the bill for Sheila, but, inevitably, as time wore on, Sheila began to see his flaws and insecurities. Moreover, Sheila's pattern in romantic relationships was to try to 'improve' her partner, edifying Jorgé about politics, correcting his grammar... and of course to improve his dick. Sheila had a compulsion to castrate Jorgé, and then complained that he fell short of the mark. Although Jorgé's penis has been surgically enhanced to give him a bigger, better imaginary phallus, all this was more of an imaginary order castration – especially given that he ended up having complications and several subsequent corrective surgeries. Jorgé, on his part, had a high-heeled shoe fetish that corresponded with his desire for Sheila as a phallic mother-figure, and although Sheila was happy to oblige in the bedroom with footwear, problems arose with her clear preference to be dominated, to be the bottom in missionary-style sex. They were both fighting, in a way, to be dominated by the other. This was quite contrary to their initial, conscious pictures of themselves, so speaking about their sexual fantasies, dreams, and the details of their sexual life was crucial for their analytic work. The formative effect of the work that I'm doing now is really rich and engaging, and continues to inspire thoughts. My book *Psychoanalysing Ambivalence*,[3] co-authored with Carol Owens, is more about trends that I hear about in the clinic. Ambivalence is also relatively under-theorised in the Lacanian world. You have to be careful to not just focus on what you are interested in in the moment in clinical work. There are certain things that show up everywhere again and again, and ambivalence is one of them! There are a number of ways to consider the concept, but the fundamental one is passed down to us from Freud when he said that ambivalence involves two equally strong 'currents' or thoughts – one conscious, the other unconscious – that cannot come up against each other. And Lacan remarks that analysis reminds us that we know nothing of love without hate. Insofar as speaking beings are split into conscious and unconscious processes, we are fundamentally ambivalent creatures. For the couple I just discussed, they were each split into a part of them that enjoyed parading as uncastrated, and a part that wanted to be castrated by the opposite sex. From another perspective on ambivalence, Carol and I hypothesise that phobia in general, and forms of xenophobia in particular, are linked to what we call an "extimate ambivalence at the heart of being". In xenophobia, one flees from the denigrated other, in order to avoid facing something disturbing about the other's jouissance – something which is ultimately reflective of the subject's own jouissance. Anyway, to circle back to what I was saying: for me, the errors and the 'I wonder what I could have done better' in my earlier work are the ones that I sort of find myself going back to – as an analyst in my formation, as a clinician – for further development. It is not that I ever stopped doing that, but those were, sort of, mini-ruptures for me that needed tending to.

DD: It's about ruptures we all too often try to avoid.

SS: For me currently, that is family therapy. It's already complex enough with couples. I don't do groups anymore either. I would like to be working with groups again, but I don't have the space for it with how my life is structured right now. Same for families, I would really need the time to do a lot more studying before I even start it in close supervision with multiple supervisors. Maybe if I had another life, or if I'd quit being an academic or something... I'm good with the wheelhouses that I currently have, and feel inspired enough to tread new grounds within the realms that I have. It is not necessarily a 'not-wanting to know', but a 'I can't know everything'.

DD: If you were to work with families, you immediately state that you would talk to a lot of supervisors. Could you tell me more about that?

SS: Sure! I was lucky enough to be able to work with – during my doctoral studies, my analytic formation with the Lacanian School of Psychoanalysis, and afterwards – a variety of supervisors. I remember saying to my husband, after a first supervision session with a new supervisor: "Wow! That was amazing." I just loved it. When someone helps me see the theory in clinical work in a way that I always knew was there, it helps to listen in a fresh way. It helped me to take up theory from a slightly new perspective, and to start intervening a little bit differently. At some point I was seeking out a different supervisor, because I was treading the same old ground – though I didn't have any patients where I thought I wasn't doing well. I just felt there was more, and I always have been a believer that supervision doesn't end when training ends. You can never see everything, nor can your supervisors. They don't have supervision. But when you are in an analytic situation, there will always be certain things that you miss. You've interviewed Annie Rogers, well, the next time I have a psychotic analysand, she's who I am going to call! In *The Unsayable* she presents a session-by-session accounting of some rich clinical cases. After the recounting of each session, she has notes about the session. Reading this with my students, I thought: "My goodness, even Annie Rogers thinks and reflects after sessions. If only I could have heard this or that, maybe I would have done certain things differently." But I heard 'this' and I intervened in 'this way', and usually that also works out.

DD: We often only know in retrospect if our interventions had a certain – good or bad – effect.

SS: Yes. Or seemed to have very little effect. In the course of every session we encounter analytic choice points, moments of deciding whether or not and how to intervene, and just like meaning can only be determined after the fact, the same is true for the effects of our interventions. I also think it's important to remember that silence is an intervention, as is the mere presence of the analyst – in whatever modality, in-person, by video or by phone. And, of course, our presence always has effects!

DD: I really like this idea of 'analytic choice points'.

SS: It's a really useful term to me. At a certain level, when we're in the position of the analyst, we're always encountering analytic choice points; that is, we're always making choices as to how we listen, and when and how to intervene. However, both during the session and afterwards, upon reflection, there tend to be certain moments we think more explicitly to ourselves that this or that was an important moment, and that there are or were several options as to how to respond. Each moment in the practice of psychoanalysis is an ethical choice. Lacan speaks in *Seminar VII*[4] about the ethics of desire, in *Seminar VIII*[5] about the atopia of the analyst's desire, in *Seminar XVII*[6] about the discourse of the analyst, and really all throughout his work about how to occupy the position of the analyst, how to practise the analyst's desire – in short, how the analyst's desire aligns with the sphere of the ethical. Each moment in the span of an analytic session, perhaps especially its scansion, is one in which the analyst chooses, both consciously and unconsciously, the way in which they take up – or not – the analyst's desire in relation to the speech of the analysand. And so, while there might be certain analytic choice points that would be identified by the structure of the session, such as how to begin – or let the analysand begin – and how to end, or might be identified by many analysts, an analytic choice point is always an individual analyst's ethical encounter with an individual analysand.

DD: Well, we're going to end on that one. Thanks a lot!

Notes

1 Swales, S. (2012). *Perversion: A Lacanian Psychoanalytic Approach to the Subject.* Routledge, New York.
2 Hook, D. and Vanheule, S. (2023). *Lacan on Depression and Melancholia.* Routledge, New York.
3 Swales, S. and Owens, C. (2020). *Psychoanalysing Ambivalence with Freud and Lacan.* Routledge, New York.
4 Lacan, J. (1986 [1959–1960]). *Le Séminaire VII: L'éthique de la Psychanalyse.* Seuil, Paris.
5 Lacan, J. (2001 [1960–1961]). *Le Séminaire VIII: Le Transfert.* Seuil, Paris.
6 Lacan, J. (1991 [1969–1970]). *Le Séminaire XVII: L'Envers de la Psychoanalyse.* Seuil, Paris.

Chapter 8

Kristen Hennessy – You Can't Do It Alone

Kristen Hennessy, PhD, is a licensed psychologist in private practice in rural Pennsylvania where she treats traumatised children from a Lacanian framework. She is the co-editor of *Psychoanalysis, Politics, Oppression and Resistance* (Routledge, 2022) and her work appears in *Lacanian Psychoanalysis with Babies, Children, and Adolescents: Further Notes on the Child* (Routledge, 2017), amongst other places.

Dries Dulsster (DD): I would first like to thank you for participating in this endeavour. I start every interview with the same question, namely: "Who is your Dora?" On hearing this question, what comes to mind?

Kristen Hennessy (KH): Well, if you ask me again tomorrow, I'll probably have another answer, but there is a case that consistently comes to mind. It's a current case, but I started working with this child when he was 8, and now he is 17. His case has had more clinical surprises than any other case I've had. The first surprise came right after he was referred to me. I said that I didn't know if I could work with him, but I decided to give it a try. I was told that he was non-verbal, and he was referred by a case worker of children and youth services. They knew that the father of this child was a sex-offender. They told me the child was non-verbal, and that he had his skull cracked open by his mother. He had just been abandoned near a park by his previous foster family, and they asked if I could work with him. I said I didn't know. I said I'd meet him, and I'd try. The first lesson here was not to listen to the referral source. So, this little boy came in, me thinking he can't speak. He was playing in my sandbox, and I was just narrating what he was doing. He was playing with this blue truck, and he would move it slowly, and I would speak slowly. When he moved it quickly, I spoke quickly. Suddenly, he turned around and he talked to me! I even remember his exact words, because I almost passed out. This little boy, who I was told could not speak, turned around in his first analytic session and said: "When I was little, it was dark. The dark made me sick. I had hiccups, I cried, and no one heard. Now, it's all in here (his head)." That was his entrance into the treatment.

DOI: 10.4324/9781003410935-8

DD: That indeed is a surprise!

KH: It was such a surprise! I remember that after that session I called the case worker that had legal custody of him. I said: "You know, he can speak!" Since then, I have been much more open to surprises. It is about being willing to allow a child not to be who I've been told that they will be.

DD: It makes me think of Freud who stated that the most successful cases are those in which we allow ourselves to be taken by surprise.

KH: Indeed. It also makes me think of psychoanalytic theory: it is a blessing and a curse. We must know theory; we must allow theory to teach us. But never at the expense of the patient, never at the cost of failing to listen. This keeps theory alive; it keeps it fresh – if what happens in my consulting room is not lining up with a particular piece of theory, I must nevertheless privilege the speech of the patient. Now, the second lesson this boy has taught me was about enduring the violence which can appear in clinical work. That sounds... well... I'm looking at your recorder, but I feel I shouldn't censor myself. You've told me I can edit it later, so I'm just going to speak freely.

DD: It indicates that free speech cannot be taped!

KH: No. It cannot be taped. I am sometimes asked if I record my sessions, and I most certainly do not! It introduces a new kind of audience in a way that is absolutely detrimental to the treatment.

DD: You said he taught you to endure violence. To me, this does not seem like an easy thing to do.

KH: I was thinking that my hesitance highlights that there's something taboo about speaking about kids with symptoms of significant violence, as though the violence ought to be censored. There is this certain fear among caretakers. As a clinician you have a responsibility for the wellbeing of the child, and the wellbeing for those around the child. As such, there can be a temptation to easily hospitalise. And I should say that I have hospitalised him. I have never put him in residential care, but I have put him in short-term inpatient care for safety for a total of three times in nine years. There certainly is a time and a place for an inpatient stay. However, he taught me to tolerate my own anxiety. He taught me to first say: "Can we make this safe?" instead of: "This child has a violent urge; we need to hospitalise him." The question is what structures we can put into place to allow the child to stay home. Allowing the child to stay home allows the treatment to continue. He taught me how to get creative with putting safety into place, so that the treatment could continue. A child needs the message: "We are not going to allow you to destroy... but we are not going to kick you out either! We're going to keep you as one of us, and this is how we are going to do it!" I remember when his mother would call me and say: "He is attacking me... can we come over?" And I would respond: "I have an opening in three hours." Then when I went into my waiting room, he would be there trying to get to her while she held the door shut from outside. But that is maintaining safety! She was safe, he was safe. She could see him through the door, so she knew he was still trying to attack her... but she also knew he was fine. And then I would get him, and we would get to work.

DD: How did you manage this violence in the sessions?

KH: Kids break my stuff a lot of times. Kids do hit me, I do get attacked, but I also learned how to respond to them. And I also practise martial arts now (*both laugh*). So, these days I'm more confident in my capacity to survive (*laughs*). I've heard that Jacques-Alain Miller said that Lacan's great strength was practising judo. I'm talking about the physicality of the violence, yes, but there is also something about martial arts that deeply ties into analytic work, of working with, rather than against, what is present in a treatment.

If they break my stuff, whatever. You know, I'm very fortunate with my landlord. Before I moved in – they are the in-laws of lawyers who represent my patients, so they kind of knew what they were getting into when I signed the lease – I said: "There are going to be holes in the walls sometimes." And they said: "Okay." They are wonderful. So now I text them: "There's a new hole" (*laughs*). If I can get a door between myself and a child that is trying to attack, that means I'm safe. But I find a lot of times that it is workable. Even with that kind of intense physical violence, there are ways into words. There are ways to endure it. When I talk about martial arts, it's more that I have learned that getting hit isn't the end of the world and if it is a 7 year old... whatever, right? We can get through this. I have learned in working with a violent child that I can use words to stop them. Maybe not to stop the violence, but to make it manageable, to get it to a level where we can continue to work. Kids, like this child, have taught me that I need to be prepared for violent outbursts in my office, and that I should structure this space accordingly. It is why I have punching gloves and a punching bag. I also don't throw boxes away. I collect them. Some boxes become art projects, but it is also what the kids are allowed to destroy. I make sure that if a child needs to destroy or attack something, we can do that safely. It is also how I structure my office in terms of what is kept where.

DD: How many holes do you have in your wall?

KH: I have had many... but currently none! Recently, I had a teenage girl who was about to put holes in the wall. That is what she does in her foster home. However, she didn't because of what I said to her. She was really trying to go inpatient, but I wasn't sending her. She then threatened she would punch holes in the wall until I would do it. She was looking at me, pulled her fist back and started hitting the wall a couple of times, until I turned to her foster mom – they were both in the waiting room – and said: "You know, my landlord has insomnia, and before I moved in, I told him this might happen sometimes. He has stuff to patch it, and he really finds this kind of project to be soothing. It might help him sleep." She sat back down. She wanted to make me angry. She didn't want my landlord to get a good night's sleep. It might have not been the most analytical thing to say, but it worked, and it kept her outpatient. It was the first time in her life she had gotten through this internal state without being hospitalised, so I consider it to be a success.

DD: I don't understand why that would not be an analytic intervention. It seems like a good example of how we should be creative.

KH: I've put it like that, because I think it is not what one would consider to be a standard analytic intervention. However, I think that what it showed her and what I was saying to her is that 'your violence doesn't scare me, you're trying to destroy all your relationships, and, by the way, you are helping this man. You do what you have to do. Come in and talk to me about it!' So yes, it was an analytic intervention.

DD: A true analytic intervention is always a creative intervention!

KH: Yes, and one should also learn to be creative together. With this case, I think I also learned about the team and the importance of the team. Foster parents can be especially important. The case I first discussed probably should have been a residential facility case, but he never went. We felt strongly about that. His story was very sexual, very violent. He had fantasies about raping and murdering babies. He was abandoned in a psychiatric hospital, and no one in the state wanted to go and pick this child up. The team got together – we had monthly meetings and we brainstormed – and we asked ourselves if there was someone who loved him. And there was this 27-year-old single woman who had been his aid at school. We called her, and we said: "Do you want to be a mom?" And she replied: "I need two days to set up a bedroom for him." She went and got him from the hospital, and she has adopted him. She is married now. She taught me about a parent's capacity to get through with a very troubled child.

DD: I would like to circle back to the idea of theory as a blessing and a curse.

KH: Yes, this child taught me that you cannot get through with just your theory, although you must have your theory. You must listen to the child.

Working with children does two things. First, it confirms theory. You do not have to abstractly believe how structure comes to form, because you can watch it unfold. It confirms psychoanalytic theory to me. However, they also present me with many inconvenient truths. When they enter your office, and they do not line up with theory, you have to listen to your patient! You can always figure out later if something does fit with theory.

DD: Maybe we could even say that for each case we have to listen to the element that does not line up with theory?

KH: Yes. The fact of the matter is that you are ethically obliged to listen to your patient. Concerning the case discussed I must say that I felt uncomfortable with a lot of things that he presented. For me, it did not line up with some Lacanian ideas, like those I had concerning dissociative identity disorder.

DD: How come?

KH: I worked with him through the hypothesis of a psychotic structure, but he also presented distinct personality states, like a dissociative personality disorder. This is a disorder I did not want to believe in. Here in the US, there is a debate concerning dissociative identity disorder. It is a question of whether it exists or if it is created by therapists. This case, and another one, prompted me to get more training regarding dissociative identity disorder. However, a lot of that training was appalling to me, and I ended up rejecting it. What I mean by that is that a lot of the training seemed to be reifying the idea of that disorder. Especially in hysterics, it creates dissociative identity disorder. So, saying to someone who presents with some kind of multiplicity: "Oh tell me about your other parts, tell me about this part..." reifies it as opposed to what I came to believe, and probably should have believed the whole time. I think I was nervous, because I did not want to be part of creating something like that in him, but I also wanted to respect what he was bringing in. What I've come to believe is that it is way easier when it does not matter if it is an 'alter'. It doesn't matter. He's bringing it in the session, so listen to it all, and it will work itself out. Nothing special needs to happen. But I think I had anxiety, because there are camps about this, and I didn't always do the things that the training concerning dissociation taught me to do, which is to specifically ask to search for dissociation and to almost encourage it. I still think like that, but then, of course, when it comes in, it comes in. What are you going to do except listen?

In addition, I had a supervisor at the time who believed that dissociative identity disorder did exist, but that it was only possible for people who are structurally neurotic. I believed that as well. And yet, the child before me was not at all neurotic at that point in the treatment, though he did present with alters. Like with theory, I needed to learn to listen to supervisors, but also to not permit that to cancel out what was happening in my office. I can't change what my patients bring into the room. He had personality states which would burn the house down. He had another state in which he would try to murder. But we still kept him home. His foster mom unplugged the oven for years though. (*laughs*)

DD: For years!?

KH: Yes! And that was not even all. The most profound commitment that I saw from her to him was when she had undergone abdominal surgery. He had hit her in her incision right after the surgery. Because of that she had to have another operation. So, we asked if we had to put him on respite, which would have meant sending him to another family's home for a period of time. She refused. She then had her surgeon build a protective case around the incision in her abdomen. This woman is now in clinical training, by the way (*laughs*). I know I'm talking about the caregivers rather than the patients for a surprising amount of time, but I can't do it alone. A lot of the kids have taught me that. I would not have been able to keep him safe on my own. I really needed him to be loved by a family to become safe. As such, he also taught me a lot about trusting the process, no matter how ugly it gets. He has not been violent in four years now. He is still a child – or a man – on the spectrum, but he is really thriving in the best way he can. He has friends now, and he enjoys relationships. He is still obsessed with cars, but everyone in his family has embraced that. The cars allowed for a social connection. So, when I have a child patient now who is incredibly violent, who is acting out sexually, this case comes to mind. I know what to do now. What I have to do is follow the analytic process. I should not panic. I should not freak out. We will get there.

DD: Something else: have you ever published something concerning those cases?

KH: No, I haven't published this case, but I think I will at some point. However, the parents and the boy gave me permission to present his case at conferences, and to use his name within our community to remind people – people on our teams, who are fearful of a child and of us – that they should stick with the work. I also used it in the treatment to show him how he evolved. It is kind of touching, because it went from talking about how you can't rape to telling him that it is okay when he wants to kiss a girl and she likes to kiss him back.

DD: That is a big difference.

KH: It is! And I love that that's what we are working on now. If she wants to kiss you and you want to kiss her... sure! Go ahead and kiss!

DD: Having to tell someone they shouldn't rape, and having to endure that kind of violence... I can imagine that not a lot of people are willing to work with these kinds of patients. However, when you talk about it, it has a very enthusing effect. Something like: 'Clinical work, come on!'

KH: Yes!

DD: You illustrate that a lot of things seem possible with those kids.

KH: Yes! And that is what I like about this work: it works! It is intense. It takes a very long time, but it can happen. It is amazing to watch those children take on those journeys. I think he and several other children have taught me to trust children. Just follow the analytic process. Allow them to have that. Make sure they have people that love them, they need that. If you give them that, it might take six years before things get better, but it will, and I have come to trust that.

DD: Learning to trust the process seems important, but it also seems like it isn't there from the start?

KH: I think it means remembering that the analytic process is possible. Lacan does not say that analysis is only available to the worried well. Speech has tremendous power. When bodies are at risk, anxiety can kick up, resistance can set in. We can be tempted to forget the power of speech, to think that 'something must be done', while forgetting that the analytic process is itself 'the something'. It is about giving treatment to the children, which is something my community helps me do. When I supervise, a lot of supervisees are talking about people who want their child to stop doing certain things. I feel fortunate that this is not how I am positioned by my community or by the people sending children to me. They allow the treatment to belong to the child, and I do a lot to try and make it happen. At the end of an intake with a kid, I will ask them if they want to come back and when. And then – even if they say they want to come back, or whatever their answer is – I will say, in front of the child, to the caregiver that they would like to come back on a certain day. If the caregiver can't or won't schedule that, that's fine, but it means that one of my first acts is the child seeing me advocate for them. And I think my community is good at not expecting treatment to be about the elimination of symptoms, but about something much more profound or transformative.

DD: So, the case of this boy taught you to not listen to the referral (yes), to be wary of theory (yes), to be able to support violence (yes) and that love is necessary (absolutely). That's already a lot for one case, but are there other cases that have had a certain impact on you?

KH: I think the first kids I saw made me think differently about working with structural diagnosis.

DD: Do elaborate!

KH: There is this one case of a little boy who was 3 when we started. He was in a foster home where he was utterly rejected, so he moved to another foster home. He had been sexually abused in ways involving food. This person would put peanut butter on his penis, and would then ask the child if he wanted a snack. This very little boy of course had no way of knowing that this was wrong. In addition, he was severely neglected by his mother. I think the mother did not want him to be alive. The boy was masturbating all the time, was trying to touch everybody sexually, but he was 3 years old, and he just... He was one of the kids who confirmed theory for me so strongly. The treatment had a very neuroticising effect on him... and he did that on his own. That was how it felt to me. It is as if I was there to provide treatment, but he just did that himself. And he would sing. He was so creative. He also taught me something that I now use very often. A kid who's been told not to talk about certain things or not to tell me specifically... Kids are so concrete, and if they want to tell you, they are willing to violate any prohibition. They might be afraid; they might even have been told they'd be killed if they told something. But it helped when I highlighted: "You promised not to tell me, but you didn't promise not to ask me, you didn't promise not to sing it." So, this little boy used singing instead. When he said he wouldn't be telling me, I replied: "Well, don't tell me, sing it!" (*laughs*). Creating a different category that still involves speech, but does not feel like what they promised not to do helps a lot. He also sang a song about this neuroticising effect. Do you know the song "There Was an Old Lady Who Swallowed a Fly"?[1] It's about something that eats a fly and then bigger and bigger animals eating the thing that ate the fly, ending with: there was an old lady who swallowed a horse... She's dead, of course!

His song was something like:

> *There was a mother who swallowed me up*
> *Kristen made her throw me up*
> *Then I made her spit me out*
> *patew, patew, patew,*
> *I'm not a food, I am a boy.*

I think that was him speaking of his process from a more neurotic position. It was instructive to me: he had been swallowed up by his mother, and it was my role to make her throw him up, but then it was his role to spit her out. I think he taught me my role versus his role in his process. I had to get him back into the mouth of the crocodile, and then – I don't know who put the wedge in there – it was his job to escape.

DD: Those cases make me think that, at a certain level, the clinical structure only gets us so far. The work happens, and, like you say, it is about following the process, following their speech, following their singularity.

KH: I also think that, when we are young... Lacan doesn't say we are born with our structure.

DD: Indeed, there is a lot of possibility. I remember you stating at the *Clinic and Culture Conference* in Pittsburgh that you must give these children a chance to use the symbolic, and see where it gets them.

KH: I see it as my job to invite them into using the symbolic, and then they do what they do. But if they haven't been invited to do so...

DD: Is there something else you would like to add?

KH: Yeah, I hope more people will work with kids, because we can do so much. It is also so fun. It is the same process, but it is different, and I love it.

DD: I agree!

KH: I think that if you are going to work with kids, you have to allow yourself to work with a team and in a community. I think all my cases show this. So, I'd say that's another thing they taught me. Confidentiality is vital, but a child needs more than their analyst, and we can be part of facilitating what they need.

DD: To wrap it up, I would say that I agree that many more Lacanians should work with children. But, as we already mentioned, it does not seem to be that easy.

KH: Yes, that's true. With adults, I don't have to say anything. I can wait. I can listen for as long as I need for some slip or something to pop up which I can then highlight. But when a kid comes in, and they are playing, and they say: "You are the dad!" – then you must play the dad. But that is where theory comes in. I will grant that those early sessions are still hard, because you don't know how to orient yourself. You are still figuring out the structure, or what your position may be in the transference, but that's where your case formulation saves you. A structural diagnosis gives you a certain orientation, while still figuring things out. During the sessions you keep changing your conceptualisation, and all the while your patient is changing too. In a certain way that's also what saves you. Like when you work with a case of perversion; I know what that means for what my role is. It allows me to be creative in play.

DD: For me, there was a time when I thought that once I had a certain idea about the clinical structure, I knew exactly what to do. This is true to some extent as it offers an orientation, but we must be careful not to ignore indications of other structures. This was marvellously illustrated by the interview with Amar. However, it does not address the singularity of each patient. At the core of it, we must be able to listen to what our patients are saying.

KH: You can't get lazy with it. You have to keep paying attention.

DD: Well, that's a very good way to end an interview. Thanks a lot!

KH: No problem.

Note

1 Ives, B. (1953). "There Was an Old Lady Who Swallowed a Fly." *Folk Songs, Dramatic and Humorous.* New York: Brunswick Records.

Chapter 9

Patricia Gherovici – A Courageous Endeavour

Patricia Gherovici, PhD, is a psychoanalyst, analytic supervisor, and recipient of The Sigourney Award 2020 for her clinical and scholarly work with Latinx and gender variant communities. She is the co-founder and director of the Philadelphia Lacan Group and Associate Faculty, Psychoanalytic Studies Minor, University of Pennsylvania (PSYS), honourary member at IPTAR, the Institute for Psychoanalytic Training and Research in New York City, and founding member of (Das) Unbehagen. She co-published *Psychoanalysis in the Barrios: Race, Class, and the Unconscious* – winner of the Gradiva® Award for best edited collection, and the American Board and Academy of Psychoanalysis Book Prize. Additionally, she is the author of *The Puerto Rican Syndrome* (2003), *Transgender Psychoanalysis: A Lacanian Perspective on Sexual Difference* (2017) and the co-author of *Psychoanalysis, Gender, and Sexualities: From Feminism to Trans* (2022).

Dries Dulsster (DD): Hi Patricia, thanks for participating in this project. When I emailed you, you responded very enthusiastically and replied: "The Dora-effect! I know that very well." So, it's not just about 'Who's your Dora?' but there's a 'Dora-effect' as well! What do you want to tell me about that?

Patricia Gherovici (PG): There is one feature I admire in Freud: with Dora, he had the courage to publish a seemingly failed case. This is the story of a case in which the analysand leaves the treatment before completing it, which leaves many questions unresolved. This is moreover a case Freud kept returning to. The narrative about Dora was not initially meant to be a case study, it was rather an addition to the *Interpretation of Dreams*.[1] It provided an example, a vignette, of how dream interpretation could be used in the progress of treatments. It only became a clinical case later. What is also brilliant, is that Freud returned to his case and rewrote it in the footnotes. In the 1920s he had progressed in his thinking about feminine sexuality, and was able to better understand where he had failed. Freud became aware of a certain heterosexist prejudice that had prevented him from being effective as a psychoanalyst. Recall that he first assumed that Dora would have to be attracted to a man!

DOI: 10.4324/9781003410935-9

The clinical richness of the case guided Freud in becoming aware that if Dora could love a woman like a man, his initial heterosexist prejudice couldn't be sustained, which collided with the clinical material. So, what occurs to me is that the Dora-effect concerns those analysands who teach us to become better analysts, or furthermore, who make us become psychoanalysts. Freud's Dora also suggests that the best way to transmit psychoanalysis is via failure. As to our positioning in the cure, one only becomes a psychoanalyst if there is an analysand that allows us to intervene in an analytic way. Thanks to transference, they position us as such. This cannot be taken for granted. You may have a beautiful office, a designer couch, somebody coming five times a week for thirty years, but that's not necessarily psychoanalysis. On the other hand, one can practise psychoanalysis in a place that is not considered traditionally psychoanalytic and may not even have a couch, as it was my experience in the barrio clinic. What matters is the type of interaction that psychoanalysis requires – analytic listening. It is the position of the analyst who hypothesises that there is a divided subject with an unconscious that allows for the treatment to be truly psychoanalytic.

DD: It came up in different interviews. We could say that the Dora-effect would be that one is able to make the switch from the master's discourse – hanging on to one's prejudices and the frame of a so-called psychoanalysis, like the number of sessions, the couch and so on – to the analytic's discourse? The switch from psychotherapy to psychoanalysis? The switch from psychotherapist to psychoanalyst?

PG: There is a moment when an unexpected truth emerges in the treatment – via a slip of the tongue, a dream, a parapraxis – that helps analysts intervene and position themselves as such. The analysand turns a corner and engages in the transference they have created – as a supposition of a subject supposed to know embodied in the analyst. One could say this transference retroactively makes of the preliminary meetings – that liminal period of elucidation and obfuscation that could look like psychotherapy – something that becomes proper psychoanalysis.

DD: And mentioning Freud, you said it takes courage!

PG: I have the experience as a supervisor and in my own practice that discussing or presenting cases is a very vulnerable, difficult thing to do. One exposes oneself every time one presents clinical material. It is sometimes an invitation for anyone who listens to occupy the position of supervisor. At times it can even be an invitation for public shaming. Often, people in the audience feel not only that they have an opinion, but that they know more and better than the analyst presenting the case; public presentations can be experienced as a scene of carnage. The presentation of the clinical material is very delicate, and it requires courage to expose one's clinical work to an audience, be it at a conference, with a supervisor, or to a group of colleagues. In this regard, Freud gave an admirable example when he chose to publish cases, even when he was left with more questions than answers. Dora had left abruptly and upset. As I said, years later, in his footnotes, Freud revised and even challenged his own position. It takes courage to expose one's blind spots to a general readership. This is something other brilliant analysts like Melanie Klein have done as well. They appear to be more in transference with psychoanalysis than the other psychoanalysts that could criticise them. They were probably aware that for psychoanalysis to progress – if we believe that psychoanalysis is a discipline that is in constant evolution – we need to be able to expose these moments of failure. We learn from the mistakes; we learn to fail better.

DD: Most of the analysts I interviewed had written about these cases or presented something, and, indeed, it takes a certain courage and desire to want to know something about these failed cases.

PG: Maybe even something of our death drive! As Sabina Spielrein put it: destruction is the cause of becoming.

DD: It exposes the things we don't want to know.

PG: Indeed, our passions: love, hate and ignorance. There is something about the process of writing out a case that allows the analyst to radically transform the understanding of a case. Writing about a case is a way to figure out what role one plays or has played in the treatment. People often go to talk to a supervisor in moments when something isn't working. The writing itself can function as what the supervisor would do – offer another vision. It would be a way of rethinking. I often ask the people who I supervise to write a page or two about the case before we meet. The writing of the case allows the analyst to revisit the case from a different angle, a different perspective. This is always productive. There is something in this writing that may help the analyst to occupy their position in a better way. In my personal experience, I work better clinically when I write about the case. It is a way of avoiding the entrapment of playing the hero. There are many written stories of psychoanalysis where it is tempting to present ourselves as a hero. As a result, there are some colleagues who are very opposed to the idea of clinical presentations, because they feel these indulge in the analyst's narcissism. Of course, the temptation to portray oneself as a hero is there: "We saved the analysand! Look at my interventions! We made them better people." And then they mount their horse, and go on to the next heroic quest. Although this danger is present, it should not restrain us from sharing cases – even at the risk of indulging in one's narcissism, for there is always a lot to learn. Beyond the courage, I admire the generosity in Freud who leaves a legacy we miss with Lacan. We don't know much about Lacan's clinical practice. It is severely limited in his publications, although he had public clinical presentations every week. We see Lacan as an analyst when he reads other people's cases, and he does it brilliantly. This loss has to do with Lacan's difficulties with writing. Lacan's style is famously challenging, dense, scientific, and poetic at the same time. His essays are reputed to be 'difficult', both concise and allusive, and often summarise in a few pages the developments of a year-long seminar. They also mirror the opaque texture of speech in a psychoanalytic cure. They challenge you, and test your desire.

DD: And we still talk about Freud's cases today! That being said, I'm going to make an appeal to your courage and generosity. Would you care to present one of your Dora's?

PG: Yes, and I have to say that there are a lot of them. Each analysand gives us a lesson about important elements like transference, resistance, the unconscious, the object *a*... Transference and resistance are the two basic elements needed if one is to have analysis. Transference and resistance are enough, as Freud said. These are the two conditions under which an analysis may start. One analysand I have in mind, Socorro, is a case I have published in several places. It is not a traditional case. Most of the time, people come to see you when they have some question about themselves. These are the conditions for the establishment of transference. They don't know something about themselves, and assume that if they consult an analyst, they will figure something out about their symptom. This motivates them as they feel that the symptom represents them. It is an enigma to resolve. The case I'm thinking of was interesting to me, because it wasn't clear what I could do with this person. I struggled with this young woman. She was 24 when she came to see me in the barrio clinic, after being given the diagnosis of PTSD. She had been the victim of a violent crime. She did not arrive with the motivation of 'I need to talk to someone, and that will help me.' This productive starting point was missing. She came to see me to pay a debt to the doctor who saved her life. She was working in a laundromat when it got robbed very late at night, and several assailants came with guns. The few people that were left in the store were ordered to lie on the ground. They went to a room in the back to take the money, and as they were leaving, they randomly shot at the people on the ground. Only one person got hit, which happened to be Socorro. She got a bullet in the head that could have killed her. She was saved by a miracle. She lost part of her hearing and a part of her eyesight. After many months of treatment, she finally went home. The doctor who had saved her recommended that she'd talk to someone. As you can see, it wasn't the best condition for treatment to succeed, because coming to see me was the doctor's wish, not hers. An analysis is a treatment by words and silence. She wasn't even talking in the beginning. She came, but was silent. Not just silent, but she was sobbing inconsolably. It was difficult. I had to trust the process: you offer the possibility of being listened to, and see whether that works. I waited, and eventually she started to speak. One thing that she said was that she was ashamed of the scar. I found that was a promising beginning.

DD: How so?

PG: Because it was her own implication in the scene of the trauma, the promise of something that could become a symptom. I disagreed with the initial diagnosis she was given, which was PTSD. I felt that we were still before the creation of trauma. This case taught me a lot. It allowed me to revisit the idea of *Nachträglichkeit*, the deferred temporality of trauma. She had a pre-traumatic stress disorder! There was no trauma yet. The analysis had to create the scene of trauma that she could traverse and then move away from. When she stated that she was ashamed of her scar, she gave me a fantastic opportunity. I saw this as an attempt to find a solution. Indeed, she was creating a situation in which she had agency, even if she was saying how ashamed she was that people would see this ugly scar, perhaps think bad things of her, or implied that she deserved to be shot. In a way she was beginning to make sense of a situation that was completely random or absurd. Why did they shoot her and not the person next to her? This was an encounter with the *tuché*, and she was trying to make sense of this Real, a violent confrontation with death. Another interesting element was her wish to hide the scar she was ashamed of. She would wear a sort of turban, a colourful wrapping around her hair, and paradoxically it called attention to what she wanted to conceal. It's like what Freud wrote about cases of a hysterical attack: one hand lifts the skirt and the other pulls it down. This contradiction is a feature that compromise solutions have. Beyond this moment of shame, she started to speak more while looking for anyone who could be found guilty.

DD: In the song "Guilty Party"[2] by *The National*, Matt Berninger sings: "There's no guilty party, we just got nothing left to say." Searching for a guilty party is a search for a cause, and it's this search that makes us speak.

PG: She was indeed searching for a reason. She felt guilty for working at a laundromat late at night. She thought that her boyfriend was guilty, because he was unemployed and did not bring in any money, which forced her to accept a bad job. Or it was her son's fault, because he happened to be there during the robbery and started screaming. Or it was the laundromat store's fault, because they did not have a better security system. It was then that she started to refer to this event that brought her to the treatment, and that had dramatically transformed her life as an 'accident.' Can we compare being shot in the head in Philadelphia's barrio to having a car crash on a highway? Since this area has very high levels of crime, was the event 'accidental'? How the event took place was overdetermined by social conditions and the inequities of life in the ghetto. The ambulance took a long time to arrive, because there were shootings almost every night in that area. Here, the etymology of 'accident' is helpful, the word derives from the Latin 'accidere' (to happen) and is etymologically akin to 'cadere' (fall). This 'fall' (cadere) is also present in the root of the word 'chance', and in the root of the word 'symptom', which in Greek literally means 'to fall together' (*syn*, with, together + *piptein*, to fall). This new verbal production corresponded to a moment in the treatment during which Socorro was suddenly able to let 'fall' the idea of finding a guilty party, of blaming it all on 'somebody's fault'. After this semantic fall, she proceeded to talk about her separation from her boyfriend, her conflicts with her son, and focused especially on her relationship with her mother. Thus, she had moved around the polysemy of the phrase: 'It's my fault.' A second time, the events started to fall into the fault lines of trauma. She had been raised by her grandmother. Her mother lived in a different city. The mother would only get in touch with her when she had some illness or if there was something wrong with her physically. This horrible situation brought her mother back into her life, and she now became devoted to her daughter. She was in the hospital night and day, praying next to her. Before, the mother would only appear when she was sick. Expectably, recurrent asthma attacks, bronchitis, digestive problems, inexplicable fevers, eczema, became the means to connect with her mother. There was a reconsideration of the scene of the trauma in view of the fundamental fantasy: 'What does the other want from me?' Whether she had some personal freedom or space to move away from that overdetermined form of interaction. As she spoke, she produced knowledge about the trauma, and asked, by the pure effect of speech, what it was that she wanted. Since speaking is always speaking to someone, and since one always receives one's own message from the Other in an inverted form – by questioning the Other's desire, she asked what it was that she wanted from herself. There was a third instance when she started to distance herself from the mother. In the beginning she could not come to the clinic alone. She was afraid and needed to be escorted. She feared that the people, who had attacked the laundromat and had not been arrested, could recognise her on the street and attack her again. She was afraid of encountering them, but she slowly gained more confidence. She started speaking more, and even brought dreams as material to the sessions. Finally, there was a moment when she talked about what she first referred to as "what happened", meaning when she was shot. She was then able to express it in a new manner, and said: "When I was shot." Even when she used the passive voice, there was an 'I' that placed her in the scene, whereas before, she wasn't there at all. Her initial feelings of shame introduced her subjectivity, granting her an illusory agency in a place or in a scene that had reduced her to a mere body lying on the ground. Racialisation reduces people to bodies. 'Barrios' are racialised locations with high levels of poverty and crime. Because of the shame, she allowed her subjectivity to emerge and assert itself. I could have said to her: "Why do you feel ashamed? You're a hero, you survived." In a way it was more productive to work on her shame, and not fall into the American optimistic spiel of: 'Oh, you're a hero, you're doing very well!' One of the most basic hypotheses of psychoanalysis is that there is a subject. Psychoanalysis begins when one can treat the other person as a subject, not as an object. In this case, the treatment started in the shock of the aftermath of tragedy, and ended with the 'ordinary unhappiness' that Freud talks about. She moved from being left literally speechless, to gain a 'little bit of freedom' – as Lacan said – as a speaking subject. Another lesson this case taught me, was that psychoanalysis is not only possible in the barrio, but also much needed. If one trusts one's desire as an analyst, something happens: it could be as simple as the invitation to speak, to say whatever comes to mind, to be listened to.

DD: Considering that this woman experienced such a horrible event, I think that a lot of people would find it provocative to say that the woman did not consult you with a trauma, but a pre-trauma. It might even be more provocative to say that the analysis had to create the scene of the trauma.

PG: I agree, but as Freud noted, you need to create an artificial neurosis to cure the analysand. Of course, one might say that the traumatic event had already happened. However, for the trauma to be constituted as such, a scene needs to be created retroactively. It's a scene that one can move away from. Without this created scene, there is no possibility of movement. The counter-example would be melancholy, where the scene is one from which the subject cannot move away. The subject identifies with the lost object. For analysands to move away from trauma, they need to recreate the traumatic scene, which offers a sort of frame they can traverse. This is the condition to overcome an encounter with an overwhelming Real, because when they frame the scene, they can move away from it and open up new configurations. They then lose the frame, but clear the path for new constructions.

DD: That's an entirely different way of thinking about trauma than a lot of psychotherapies nowadays.

PG: Absolutely! Nowadays, trauma seems to be a rock, an immovable thing: "You're traumatised!" For some people this is true, and they indeed cannot overcome trauma. Others survive horrendous lived experiences, find themselves in terrible situations, and manage to go on living. If we believe that trauma would be this immovable reality, then there is no way of overcoming it. There would be no 'after the trauma'. That doesn't mean that a person who has gone through trauma will continue life without marks of that event. Of course, traumas leave marks; it is in the etymology of the word 'trauma': it means 'wound'. Wounds can heal – they leave scars, but they heal. The traversal of trauma is not a repudiation of the past, but the emergence of something new. To return to Socorro, at the end of the treatment she no longer hid the 'ugly' scar that became less conspicuous.

DD: A remark that seems to emerge in different interviews is that one 'must learn to trust the process' or 'trust in the conditions of psychoanalysis'.

PG: Yes, because you work with the hypothesis of the unconscious, and hope it will emerge. One can only operate as an analyst if the analysand ascribes you to this role. Again, what matters is not the number of weekly sessions or even if there is a couch. This is why you have preliminary sessions. You first meet the person and see if they can or want to do this type of work. If they give you the role, then you can play. It is like a casting for a play. You go to a casting, and if they think you can play the part, they give it to you. Then you play the analyst. It's staging a scene; a scene one can eventually exit.

DD: As you indicate, the preliminary work is essential for the analytic process.

PG: Yes, and in this preliminary work, Socorro needed to separate from the demand of the doctor saying: "It will be good for you to talk to someone, you're traumatised." Maybe the doctor was upset too. The whole story was very upsetting. A young woman, who had a young child, was shot in the head and had almost died. I was also moved when I heard her story, but I chose to contain my own anxiety and upset, hoping that my silence could work as an invitation. My silence was not just to let her talk, but also to offer a space where she could hear herself while talking. That is something very important in analysis. People say: "Oh well, you could talk to a friend." But what is unique in psychoanalysis, is that when you talk to a friend, you don't listen to yourself. In analysis, you are, as it were, talking like you would with a friend, but all the while listening to yourself differently, because you are talking to an analyst. There is a qualitative change. Your own words acquire a different resonance.

DD: You stated this woman was very silent. This made me think about a question that I get a lot from students: "You're into psychoanalysis and free association, and patients have to talk, but what if they come into your practice and say nothing? What if they stay silent? What do you do then?"

PG: Socorro was silent or was sobbing uncontrollably. I wondered whether I should hug her, but if I had done that, it would have originated from my own anxiety. In that case, I would have not maintained an analytic position. But one can do little things while respecting the frame. You don't need to be cruel! I handed her paper napkins in a gesture of empathy. I acknowledged she was crying and upset, but did not hug her. Such a gesture may have prevented her from speaking. The distance I kept was meant to create space, a space in which she would be free to speak or remain silent. Eventually she did start to speak – which was her choice, not mine. The fundamental rule of free association is an invitation to say whatever comes to mind, and it is an invitation for something to happen, whether it does or not. It reminds me of one of Lacan's clinical presentations. This is an interview with a patient that he calls a 'Lacanian psychosis'.[3] At the beginning of the presentation, confronted with a big auditorium, the person was overwhelmed by the conditions and remained silent. Lacan asked: "Am I doing something that is preventing you from speaking?" Lacan shows that we have a responsibility when the analysand doesn't speak.

DD: When you started talking about this case, you mentioned there were a lot of Dora's. Maybe you would be interested in discussing another one?

PG: I would like to mention an encounter that made me elaborate on trans experiences. It is because of this analysand that I had a new perspective on something I often heard in my clinical practice: analysands who identified as *cis* women – who had been assigned female at birth and thought they were heterosexual – and were posing questions about their gender identity based on same-sex sexual fantasies. Concretely, they were asking: "Am I straight or bisexual?" Some were involved in heterosexual relationships, but had fantasies about being with a woman. Some even had sexual experiences with a woman. I contrasted their questions with the experiences of some trans-identified analysands I had in my practice. I will mention one that I will call Hera, like the Greek Goddess, who was an African-American trans woman. She believed that trust was a commodity she couldn't afford. I replied: "Oh, is trust a commodity then?" And she replied: "Yes, I shouldn't be wasting your time, nor mine." Hera's comment corresponded to a current assumption about the commodification of issues like love, sex, gender, body appearance and even gender transition. It was important for me to state the obvious, that feelings are not commodities, because there is an ideological illusion that commodification frees us. But Hera also confirmed something that I encountered in the practice with trans-identified analysands. More often than not, behind a question that presented itself as an initial gender and problem of sexuality, there was something else at stake: how to find a way of existing in the world? How to find a way of being alive? How to make life liveable? Hera had been assigned male at birth, and had been a person who had experienced homelessness for a while. She grew up as a boy and went to school. In high school she met her girlfriend. They got married very young after Hera joined the military, and then at some point, while still in her heterosexual marriage, she began to have sexual fantasies during sex with her wife that they were two women having sex. She also started to wear women's clothes during sex. Eventually she wanted to take "the whole package", as she called it, and become a woman full-time. Because of this, a lot of conflict emerged in the marriage. They ended up divorcing, and Hera left the city where they were living. She moved back to Philadelphia and got a job, but she was not paying child support. One day the police showed up at her job site. This precipitated a terrible situation for Hera that triggered a psychotic episode. She left her job, abandoned all social interactions with friends, and literally went underground. She moved to the basement of her parents' home and stayed there for months. Eventually, she emerged from that being buried-alive-situation, and came to the clinic. I learned from Hera that she had found herself confronted with a situation where she had felt unable to go on living. During that psychotic episode, she told me it was the first time that she had started thinking about death and considered suicide. It was a very humiliating moment, catastrophic.

When we started working together, she was already doing better, and it appeared that she was satisfied with her hormone replacement and that the gender confirmation surgery was something that she preferred to accomplish in the future. It seemed an important strategy of deferral – postponing the gender realignment was Hera's way of imagining the future, like perspective in a painting. She would often say: "One day I'll do the surgery, and I'll be happy." It was a project to sustain her on the side of life. But the way she said it once contained a revealing slip of the tongue: instead of "I will make it happen", she said: "I will make it happy." This suggested to me that she was ascribing the formula for happiness to the surgery, which is a quite common aspiration in the US. One sees this eudaimonic idea everywhere: 'Have a gender transition, and you'll be happy!' This reminds me of Andrea Long Chu, a trans woman and an activist. She wrote an op-ed in the *New York Times*[4] saying: "I want a vagina. It will not make me happy, but I want it anyway." Happiness shouldn't be a social mandate. There is something interesting in the US: one of the rights granted to American citizens in the declaration of independence is the pursuit of happiness – transforming happiness into a commodity. Hera was not a naïve optimist, as she said once: "People talk about seeing the light at the end of the tunnel, but one should be careful – it might be the 6:15 train!" In all those sexualities in transit, the question is whether one can find oneself back on the platform, rather than on the tracks, when the train arrives. What I learnt with Hera, is that often the transgender experience is presented as a commodification of happiness. For her, postponing the surgery was a way of creating a sense of the future. What I learnt listening to Hera, was that she had found a singular strategy according to her unique mode of desire, a continuous solution to make life liveable.

DD: It's a good example that it's not because somebody talks about being trans or suggests they want to have surgery, that you should immediately push them into transitioning.

PG: Well, of course, the analyst should not be called to give approval or disapproval. We are not, and should not, be gatekeepers.

DD: I think the difficult thing is that when someone asks for surgery or keeps talking about it, one could ask: "Why do you keep postponing, isn't it time to finally have the surgery done?"

PG: It would not have been what she wanted at the time. What Hera created was a promise in the future, and the idea of 'one day it will happen'. Clearly, she was choosing to talk to an analyst to figure out what to do. She knew that other resources existed, but she was in a situation in which the surgery could take place, but later – 'not today, maybe tomorrow'. This allowed for a tomorrow to exist. I think that it is important for a trans person to have the right to make their transition in a singular manner. I think that having that choice available is a human rights issue. It's something that I hear a lot: "If I would not have transitioned, I would have killed myself." At times this could entail a transition with hormones, at times hormones and gender confirmation surgery, at times a change in pronouns. Above all, you realise that what we are talking about, beyond gender or sexuality, is finding a way to exist and survive in the world. However, it must be a decision that comes from each person choosing for themselves. It puts things in a different context when a person feels they will die if they don't transition. We must respect subjective choices. They should not be imposed by an institution or an analyst.

DD: Could you elaborate a bit on the idea that 'you heard something new'?

PG: I heard something new from analysands that I would call hysteric, like Dora, who were asking: "Am I straight or bisexual?" At first, I thought: "Oh, they read a lot of Judith Butler." Butler is the philosopher who, three decades ago, proposed that gender is performative, that it is an imitation for which there is no original – an imitation of an imitation. Butler's contentions freed gender, and even sexuality, from any biological determinism or social essentialism. My analysands suffered from an issue of gender identity, not knowing whether they were straight or bisexual. Psychoanalysis exposes the traps of identity, because the truth of the subject emerges when identity fails or falls. Why does who you have sex with determine your identity? You have a fantasy, you may realise that fantasy or not, why does it have to determine your identity, and, in some cases, cause suffering? The question 'Am I straight or bisexual?' reminded me of the classical hysterical questions that brought psychoanalysis into existence: 'What is a woman? Am I a woman?' Freud discovered that there were questions of sexuality and sexual identity behind hysterical symptoms. We also see that concern in how Lacan theorises hysteria: 'Who am I? A man or a woman? What is to be a Woman?' These are the hysterical questions par excellence. These questions are also key in the case of Dora. And this very question was formulated in an original way. It was no longer: 'Am I a woman? What is a woman?', but rather: 'Am I straight or bisexual?' I take hysteria here as a form of discourse, as a mode of social link, that is not just a neurotic structure, but that also functions as a social barometer. Something was changing in the cultural discourse about how we viewed sexuality. In the case of trans analysands, their experiences made me rethink that hysterical question in parallel with the actual suffering of trans analysands. Here, the body contradicted how they saw and felt themselves to be. In that sense it is not the question, but rather the answer that is the problem. But it was also about finding a way to exist in the world. Concerning Hera, during the time we worked together, she felt comfortable in her gender without needing the surgery; taking hormones seemed to be enough at the time. She was living life as a woman, and her gender transition 'as a work in progress' appeared as a way to stay alive in a more inhabitable body.

DD: A way of staying alive, indeed! To wrap things up a bit: do you have some final remarks?

PG: I want to say that I am grateful to the Dora's! Let them multiply! I think as long as we have Dora's in treatment, there will be psychoanalysis.

DD: That is a very good way to end the interview! Thanks a lot!

PG: You're welcome!

Notes

1 Freud, S. (1953 [1900]). *The Interpretation of Dreams. Standard Edition, IV.* The Hogarth Press, London.
2 *The National* (2017). *Guilty Party. Sleep Well Beast.* 4AD, London.
3 Lacan, J. (1980 [1976]). A Lacanian Psychosis: Interview with Jacques Lacan. In Schneiderman, S. (1980). *Returning to Freud: Clinical Psychoanalysis in the School of Lacan.* Yale University Press, New Haven, CT, 19–41.
4 Long Chu, A. (2018). My New Vagina won't make me Happy. *The New York Times,* November 24. Available at: https://www.nytimes.com/2018/11/24/opinion/sunday/vaginoplasty-transgender-medicine.html

Chapter 10

Jamieson Webster – Things We Don't Talk About

Jamieson Webster is a clinical psychologist and psychoanalyst in private practice in New York where she works with children, adolescents and adults. She teaches at The New School for Social Research and Princeton University and supervises graduate students through City University's doctoral program in clinical psychology. She is a founding member of Das Unbehagen, an organisation that explores psychoanalysis outside of an institutional or organisational framework. She has written for *Apology, Cabinet, The Guardian, The Huffington Post, Playboy, The New York Review of Books, The New York Times*, and for many psychoanalytic journals. She is the author of *The Life and Death of Psychoanalysis* (2011), *Conversion Disorder* (2018) and *Disorganisation and Sex* (2022).

Dries Dulsster (DD): So, Jamieson, thanks a lot for participating. This is the final interview. So, for the last time I get to ask: "who comes to mind when we talk about our Dora-cases?"

Jamieson Webster (JW): It immediately makes me think of two cases. I'll start with the oldest one. It was an 8½-year-old child I saw named Mariah. In a way, I thought it was a failed treatment. I did a lot of work with her, and she was intense. She had a very brutal history. Her mother was still in jail when I was seeing her, and her father had just gotten out of jail. She had been left with her paternal grandmother, and her father wasn't spending time with her; he was selling dogs, and was with a woman somewhere out of state. Mariah had questions about what men and women want. She was asking about this through an enormous amount of violence, and in the sessions I was always containing this violence. She threw my shoes down the stairwell, and locked me out of the room. We would play these games that were always on the verge of destroying the room. Something was always out of balance. I was always afraid she was going to hurt herself or me or break something. But she always had this intense question: "Why do my parents have a child, what did they want?" I remember she took this play Stouffers Stuffing box. You probably don't know what this is…

DOI: 10.4324/9781003410935-10

DD: It's an enigma for me.

JW: ... but it is a Thanksgiving item, important in the USA as a dish; the box is iconic and has classic Americana stuffing on it (*laughs*). She took this box and said: "Oh, look how nice it is to have food", and then she looked at the box, opened the top, and it became a mouth. "Oh, look, this is my father, what does he want?" And then she opened the box, and she started to stuff things from the room in it. She put make-up in it: "Men like make-up!" And then she stuffed food in it and shouted: "Women!" She just shoved all these things in the box, and I remember looking at it, thinking that the box of stuffing was stuffed with things – the stuffing that you eat became a mouth that you stuff, and just having this moment of a sense of absolute condensation. The condensed way in which she questioned why her parents had her, was how the treatment was. Every session was about this question; this compact asking which I had to tolerate. I also learned from her to not do stupid 'therapisty' things.

DD: Therapisty?

JW: Yes. For example, her dad was supposed to come visit her, but didn't. And I said something like: "You must have been disappointed", and she would just knife me. Why would you want to make the lack lack? Why do you want to be the agent who points out the lack she's well aware of? She would say, in a manner of words: "Don't pretend that you have sympathy or understand anything about me." I found that very powerful, to just shove me like that. The reason I think of her as a Dora, is because the treatment ended when I graduated and had to leave the clinic – there wasn't a way to keep it going. I tried to get her to follow me into the next clinic I was in, but it was far away. It was not in the neighbourhood, and it was outside of this people's purview. I felt terrible, because I wanted to keep working with her. Five years later, I got a call from her grandmother, and she said: "I need your help, Mariah broke a girl's arm. She is going to drop out of school, and I don't know what to do." And I thought: "Fuck." I met up with her, but it was clear that she wasn't going to come back to treatment. She didn't actually want to see me, she was just doing her due diligence in showing up, though there was still something. We looked at each other and said "Hi!" What she then told me in that session was that, yes, she had broken that girl's arm, but she had deserved it – of course.

DD: Of course!

JW: The girl had insulted and threatened Mariah, and then Mariah showed her who was boss. But that wasn't the real story. What was actually going on was that Mariah was in love with a boy, and they were having a passionate relationship. She had very much become part of his family. She wanted to quit school and start working, and be with him and his family. His family supported her and were willing to let the two of them live together in the family's house. She was pleased that she had found this family for herself. And I thought: "That's all right, this is pretty good." I wouldn't have known whether something like this was possible for her, given where she came from. So, I was really surprised by this. I said that I understood what she wanted, and that I would communicate to her grandmother that I thought her plan was sound. And she said "Okay" and left.

DD: She had taught you not to do the 'therapist' intervention or she'd knife you.

JW: And that is what makes me think of Dora.

DD: It is a very interesting thing to elaborate on. You kind of started your clinical practice with the idea to do certain therapeutic interventions, but then you stopped doing that because of her.

JW: I think because of her, and because of what children force you to do – to stay in the play with them. They don't like it when you leave the play. You try to talk about their life – someone who's life is really difficult – but she wanted to ask it the way she needed to ask it in the sessions, with and against me, through playing or various games. When difficult questions around sexuality came up, it became clear she was looking at pornography and had been exposed to a lot. She would bring up these stories: "I saw a condom thrown on the ground, and I saw this man behind a woman at the sink. What was going on there?" I remember my supervisor saying: "Just say that it is really confusing." You look and you look, and you try to understand what they are doing and what is happening, and we are not really sure what we are looking at, but we are trying to figure something out. The supervisor indicated it was a way of staying with her questioning. That was helpful, because I think with adults – I started with children and later moved to adults – you can very quickly get into a kind of therapeutic discourse, because they themselves come up with it, especially at this point in time where there are so many self-help books and memes about what a reflective 'psychologically minded' life is supposed to be. I love the children, because they don't seem to buy any of this.

DD: Working with adults is safer, children don't give you that safety. It's something that was really emphasised in the interview with Kristen.

JW: No, they don't. They teach you a lot about your limitations. You confront the impulse to want to care for them and mother them in some way. You also want to try to force the parents to be better parents, and you have to accept at a certain level that you can't. You have to accept that their life is their life, and that is hard. You must also have empathy for the parents, and not get into a place where you think that you would have done it better or that you would have been a better person. I found that very useful. At the time, I started reading Maud Mannoni, Rosine Lefort and Françoise Dolto. I found Lacanian child analysis of that period so inspiring – especially the way they differentiate maternal care. I was particularly interested in how maternal care offers oneself as a body to the body of the child around a question of satisfaction, and in what analysis has to be about and what can be done within the limits of language, and also in the way this brings critical losses and separations to bear. All of this is hard as an analyst to learn in the beginning.

DD: I completely agree. Now, there was another case as well?

JW: Yes, I saw a patient for whom the handling of transference was just *so* tough. It was someone who had already had a long analysis before me. His first analysis helped him to get away from a very symbiotic relationship with his mother, but had the problem that there was a certain limitlessness in the analysis. He consulted his analyst very frequently, and this analyst let him do whatever he wanted. He relied on his analyst for a lot of different choices in his life. It was clear that I had to set a certain limit to this. Now, creating an analytic frame with him was extremely difficult. He fought it to the nail, every step of the way. Even after a couple of years, he still tried to put everything into a transference battle. I remember this one time when he had made a slip of the tongue and associated on it, while simultaneously forcing me through questioning my desire: "Is this what you want? All the things that I've been saying aren't important to you, just this slip of the tongue?" There was always this contradiction in working with him. There would be a moment that felt important, as if to finally set a frame for analysis, but it is not as if I hadn't been doing analysis. It was difficult to find a way not to engage in this battle, but also to not disengage from it. This was a real struggle, but I learned a lot from it, and it has helped me with other cases. He was always putting me in this place of "what is your commitment?" I could've said: "My commitment isn't to my method, it is to you." But this was a problem at the same time, because I still had to direct the treatment.

DD: What exactly do you mean when you say that this is a problem? We could say that it's a good thing that you aren't so committed to your method!

JW: Yes, of course it's a good thing. Every case should make you question your method. But you should also have an idea of the frame and the direction of the treatment, and hold a certain line or limit in the interest of the work. This can change, should change, especially in tone and interpretation, but nevertheless one doesn't start working from zero. Especially in this case that had already had an analysis that had brought certain gains, but had left a whole field untouched regarding a question of separation. The first analyst allowed a kind of symbiosis between herself and the patient, which had helped wrench him out of a horrific situation that was killing him, but was itself still within the realm of a fusion. Difference, limit, and separation were shattering for this patient, and yet it was what he needed the most and fought against the hardest. Not letting him crash the boundaries of the sessions at all points in time was an unbelievable struggle. In the background of this has been the necessity to hear something of the father in a case so dominated by the mother. The father really had been pushed out of the frame of his life. So, we worked on bringing the little bits of it back here and there, in the crevices. It is funny, because Freud's Dora starts with the father and goes to Frau K., and I would say this is the reverse. It starts with Frau K., and it goes to the question of the father, and the mourning of the father. His father is interesting, because he had been eviscerated by the mother and needed to be re-found. What does Lacan say? Dora's father is an ex-soldier, a soldier with retirement papers, meaning a father who has been out-of-action and who she props up. My patient's father was very successful, but in his time with my patient he was already retired and had had many, many wives and lives. An uber-man who had mistresses in his 80s, but at the same time the father was someone who he mostly witnessed the loss of through ageing. The mother took him away from the father, and when he came back, he was an old and different man. He was the only one who really saw it that starkly. How do you wrestle with that? With the father who disappears from himself? Through handling the transference in the way I did, the father was finally able to appear, and he did elaborate on what he loved about this man which calmed down a lot in the analysis. It was as if I was making space to hear something about that which was beyond the mother, to get past what was too Real in the transference: he was continually burying this man who did actually have symbolic weight. And we found out what his father meant to him, and reconstructed his history along these lines.

DD: You talk about the link with Dora and the transference towards the analyst. The knifing makes me think of the case of Emmy, who said to Freud: "When are you going to start listening to me?"

JW: Yes, well, the man I've just been telling you about was always like: "You're not listening! I don't think you're understanding!" I just said: "I'm probably not, help me." I had to play with my lack a lot in these moments. With others, I might not do that. I like it when they say: "Shut up!" I think that on the one hand I've had a very classical Freudian training. I will allow myself to speak more at the beginning of the treatment, and will introduce silence more than others. But I also let the patients push me into silence. I can also be annoying and talk a lot, so that they push me into it.

DD: Something else that struck me during the interviews was that most of the cases compelled the analysts to write about them. Is that something that was true for you as well?

JW: Yes. I think the book about conversion disorder came out of a certain despair and need to write. I talk a little bit about that in the book, and face the conundrum of the confidentiality of the analyst; the things that I hear the most are things that are very hard to talk about. One's relationship to one's body, the drive, the erogeneity of the body, the libidinal attachment as experienced in the body... and the way this moves or transforms in analysis. It is also very difficult to write about, because the patients will recognise themselves. They can know themselves with respect to details. I think it is difficult for the patient to confront themselves objectified which is an unavoidable aspect of writing about their body and enjoyment. It is a very hard thing to put before one's analysands or patients. It is like in Freud's case with Dora when she is touching her reticule, and he says: "You're masturbating!" It was already offensive in the moment for him to point this out to her. She was angry about it! And to then write about it on top of it... I'm talking about that kind of difficulty. This whole book is a way of trying to find a way to write about cases without writing about cases per se.

DD: You mention a certain despair.

JW: I mean the despair about the loneliness of being an analyst in that respect. The part of being compelled, for me, is to get out of the loneliness, and to put something down that is not just you sitting with a patient. That is also why you question your need to write – are you trying to get out of the transference? You have to ask yourself a question when you want to write, but regardless, it is very lonely being an analyst, especially in your early career when you start to see many, many patients on your own.

DD: Could you elaborate a bit?

JW: I started seeing patients in 2001, so it's been twenty-one years. But let's say fifteen years of private practice. There is something I can do now that I couldn't do before. It is a certain way of functioning: when the patients walk into the room, it is as if the filing cabinets are there. All the material is there. When they leave, it's gone. I think it takes you a while to be able to do that. The period between starting a private practice, seeing more patients, getting to the point where I understand what it means to hold this material, but also feel okay putting it away, to have the faith that it is there, and that you can handle the work – all of that takes a lot of time, a lot of experience.

DD: And a lot of analysis. It makes me think of a moment where I asked my analyst how he could remember all of this, to which he responded: "I have no reason to forget."

JW: Ah, so getting to the point where you have no reason to forget your patient's material! And of course, there's the matter of supervision. When I experienced a lot of weight on my shoulders, I felt the loneliest. And that is often when you don't have supervisors anymore.

DD: How so?

JW: In the beginning of my training as a psychologist and psychoanalyst, I was seeing so many supervisors! We had to see three or four in graduate school. In analytic training you had one per analytic case, and then maybe you saw somebody else for the rest of your cases. There were always four people I was talking to, and who were bearing some of the responsibility, but there comes a moment when you must stop, I think.

DD: I often wonder how young clinicians manage without analysis or regular supervision. For me it has been very important to be able to do this kind of work.

JW: They are very important. I think there is the danger of drifting into the solipsism of your own practice. I think you could get lost, not knowing the boundaries or limits, and not having a place to speak. We all know that magical experience where you speak about it in a supervision group, or with a supervisor, and the case suddenly changes the very next session, without having 'implemented' anything. It makes you wonder what would happen if you never spoke about a case. All that being said, you also need to have the experience of jumping off alone with the patients for a while. It's an incredible balancing act.

DD: About seeing different supervisors. I went to a supervisor for years, someone who I think knows how to read cases in an extraordinary way. When I switched supervisors, I met someone who, after I was discussing a case of a woman who I had been seeing for seven years said: "Well, it's a bit early to say what's going on", and ended the session. It had a very important effect on me.

JW: The supervisors who teach you to listen and construct a case, and those who confront you with the limits are interesting to me. Sometimes they are the same person, but not always. But something else concerning the Dora's just occurred to me... There's an added problem when you become an analyst for people in the field.

DD: Do tell!

JW: Well, I wonder… Freud did not write about it much, but there was a time when he was seeing everybody around him. We have the letters from Ferenzci, from Marie Bonaparte. I wonder what this was like for him. And in the context of his own political infighting? As someone who sees people in the field, it is hard. People say you must have a certain kind of training to become a training analyst. That's how they talk about it, but that training is just more support for work that needs to find its frame; and you should be careful around the extra analytic contact and the spaces for that. One of the things I've seen is that analysts act out in relationship to one another. When someone finds out that someone is your patient, they often attack you to the patient. But you are the analyst, and you have to field this information. You should not react to it. You are bound by confidentiality. It is not like you can run to a friend, and say: "Fuck you!" It is interesting to hold all of that in the case of a treatment. I think a lot of the boundary violations, problematic infighting, and viciousness in institutes happens because they are not able to separate out the analysis of trainees from what they find out about colleagues or friends, and all the gossip and attacks transmitted through patients. The empathy should be on the side of the analysand for whom it is all too close, and who is placed in this problematic crossroads. At the same time, they have to find their place as an analyst amidst all of it. What a task!

DD: You state that analysts act out in relationship to one another, or they attack you towards your patient. Any idea why they do this?

JW: The only answer I've come up with is, sadly, envy. Perhaps explained by something unresolved in their own analysis, which drives them to undermine other analyses. But to be fair to everyone, transference is hot and will always be hot. What did Freud say? We should not expect to remain unscathed.

DD: How do you manage those things? How did you *learn* to manage those things?

JW: You have to figure out what to do. Classical institutes often treat the problem as something you can talk about with your patient in relation to the transference; a kind of meta-transference interpretation. But I think this is a disaster. It is a meta-cognition like any other, but it is a particularly dangerous one since it solicits the would-be-analyst onto the side of the analyst – let's 'understand' this together, you and I, we know this is 'transference'. For example, maybe another Dora… I had this analysand with whom I had some acquaintances in common, and the object voice was very important for him. The voice, which in a certain way you also withhold in the treatment, came back in the form of hearing me present papers or hearing me talk at social events. It was a question of how to make the voice disappear, because its presence was making the frame uncertain. It became clear that he was using my voice and speech to orient himself in life in an imaginary way that was stalling the analysis. I figured out a way to make my voice disappear more, and I remember him finally crying out: "Where are you, where am I, where are you, I can't hear you." It is so funny to think that institutes imagine you can solve this set of problems by talking about transference with their patients. In this case, listening to my talking was the symptom! It's always a potential symptom, especially in psychoanalytic circles where the analysts are more silent than most all day, talk too much when they get together, gossip, lecture, present. It's endless. The voice or presence of the analyst is a problem for analysts in training. It sounds so basic when you say it like this, but...

DD: I'm grateful that you've mentioned this, because I've never discussed this with anyone before. It's a thing hardly anyone mentions. A lot of psychoanalysts know one another; we know the analysts of others; some analysts are friends... Oh, and the younger ones all like to talk about their own analysis to one another!

JW: Incest!

DD: Yes, and it brings about certain problems. There's the advice, already stated by Freud, not to discuss one's analysis with others.

JW: Again, it's not like the great hysterics that keep you on your toes. This is a problem of the training of analysts. It is a problem that we should take very seriously as analysts for the future of analysis. *This* really has to keep you on your toes. You can pretend that it is fine, that this is just part of the professional life of the psychoanalysts, that we can go to the meetings and exist together in these institutes – but that's not the case. Something has to be invented or re-invented here. At least in the US, the institutes are riven with ethical boundary violations.

DD: Now, circling back to the Dora's, I don't know if something else comes to mind?

JW: I thought about one thing that happened which I thought was funny, and really surprised me. This happened some years ago, I was already studying Lacan, which I thought was very canny. I was still young, but I still can't believe that this surprised me as much as it did. I was seeing this patient, who was the first man that I saw, and my first kind of erotic transference. I was negotiating this. He was interesting. His family took part in the revolution in Iran. He had witnessed this as a child, and he had a question about what he had seen, what was exciting about it, and who his father was in relation to it.

But also about the brutality of it all, and what he was running away from. That culture also has a real stigma attached to psychotherapy, and it was hard for him to be in session with me. Because he had some connections at the college I worked at, he knew the place. One time, I couldn't see him because the college in question was closed, so he called me and said: "I can find us a room at the graduate centre." I called my supervisor, who I was very close to, and broke down crying though I didn't know why. He asked: "What is the problem?" And I said: "He said he can get a room!" And then I suddenly heard myself. It was just so funny! I really had no idea what I was so hysterical about. But I always remembered it. Just to think about how a patient can have an impact on you, and you don't know why. You are just in some kind of affective state.

DD: You, speaking out to the supervisor…

JW: That made me hear myself. And then it was no big deal anymore. You just say: "No, we're not going to get a room, we'll meet next week." But the erotic transference, we always must remember, is Real. It's Real love. So even just being the object of it for the first time can affect you in a very powerful way. I think I felt guilty. As if I must have led him to believe it was okay to say this to me. Of course, he wasn't really saying anything, he was even not aware of his act of chivalry and seduction, but I gave the truth to the lie in my sudden outburst to my supervisor, who, I must admit, I had my own erotic transference with.

DD: I have to say that you mention a lot of things we, as analysts, almost never talk about. The loneliness, the problem with knowing one another, the erotic transference from our patients and how this affects us, as well as the erotic transference we ourselves can experience. However, I think it is important. Do you want to add something?

JW: I think that I want to mention that as an analyst, one needs to feel freer. I have students who are really obsessed with the patient coming or cancelling, or paying or not paying, or talking or not talking. I don't know what this obsessionality is. I suppose they are scared, and they need their income, or they want to know what is happening with their schedule. I think they really need to get out of this problem. They should hold on to the idea of speaking and dreaming and associating. We all know this is hard. It is not that someone can do it, but that you are working towards it. You are working towards the events that allow it to take place, and to feel freer to try to move from one to the other, to put one more into place than the obsession with the schedule. It doesn't mean that you don't pay attention to it, and it doesn't mean that you don't care about that aspect of it. I went through so much training. I went through a crazy orthodox Freudian training, which was incredibly rigid, and I hated it. I have a lot to say about why I hated it, but it was also important to me. And so, I get worried. These students have a rigidity that I want to open up, but they don't have the experience this kind of orthodox training forces upon you through a strict analytic frame that I both appreciate *and* eventually had to work my way out of. However, it allowed me to understand what was possible. I wonder if a part of the rigidity of some candidates is because they have never gone through that. They are finding a different rigidity; a sort of frame rigidity against the rigidity of an analytic method which you learn to open up...

DD: It's choosing the safety of the master's discourse instead of the analytic's discourse.

JW: Yes, I have the same wonder about Lacan, because, you know... Lacan is such an incredible reader of psychoanalysis in the early part of his career, and he was classically trained. He didn't write during that time. He put his head down, and he did it. He had a classical psychiatric training, he had a classical Freudian training, and then he was able to be Lacan. In the later stages, he did something else, but you can't just start off by being a crazy late Lacan! Do you know what I mean? What is valuable there, for me, is something of an experience after running a long analysis. Seeing where patients can go, but also how long it takes them to get there – the careful work. You can't just jump to interpretation as only nonsense speech. You can't just jump to the interpretation in the mode of punning. You can't just begin by making all kinds of cuts – or you can, but people experience the analyst in utterly different ways, so one has to start in utterly different ways. I don't know what this means for our field, but I worry about it. However, it is very hard for me to say to someone: "Well, go torture yourself in a Freudian institute for six or seven years, and then let's talk."

DD: It reminds me of something a friend of mine said concerning his training in an institute: "You have to go through it to get rid of it, that's how you grow." It's saying to someone "Go torture yourself..."

JW: You know, we took these process notes, five sessions a week, as close to verbatim as possible. We did this for years. I was annoyed, because I felt like they were not listening to the signifier, so what was the point of such an extreme practise? But there is something to the rigorous method of forcing yourself to write it all down as best you can – even if they don't listen, you confront yourself as an analyst. The patients who teach you, the patients who are hard – I love the hysterical patients, obviously – they keep you on your toes, and that's thrilling. The secret problem is the deadening patients. The dead treatments. We could say the obsessional treatments. Four times a week they come and talk, and I don't know what I did. There are a couple of moments where you felt something, a surprise, but that's it. These are very hard to talk about. I've talked to some supervisees about this, and then they say: "There is one that I don't talk about." I urge them to talk about it anyway, and then they get interested in the patient again for a second, only for it to go back to the same dead place.

DD: Obviously, Dora is about a hysteric patient... I suppose obsessionals teach us a lot as well, but they make it dead.

JW: They make it dead. And hysterisation is very hard. I mean, we talk about hystericising the obsessional, but why don't we talk about how hard that is, and what else we can do? We know that Lacan cutting the session was designed to try and wake this dead thing up. But I think that I feel too scared to do it.

DD: To cut off the sessions?

JW: No, not to cut off the sessions, but to do more. You know, because they will close the box entirely, so you're walking a very fine line.

DD: It's a difficult thing to do. Maybe the next book should be: 'Who's your Rat Man?' and see what we can learn from that!

JW: Although the Rat Man was great. He was in a delirium. He came in the moment of experiencing jouissance, so there was something open about him. It immediately brings to mind this treatment that I was thinking about. He kept saying: "I was on a gurney, and I think you were there. My face was a rock and I had a rock for a face. My face was made out of rocks." That was one of the few times I woke up, because that was such a crazy image, and indeed, he is, this guy was stoned. It is about how to scale or crack the surface.

DD: Like Lacan said: the obsessional is a 'fortification à la Vauban'!

JW: Indeed, which is a rock as well. And you can climb that rock, there is some hope there. He was funny... And he got funnier throughout the treatment. I would sometimes read his sessions and think that he was so sweet. But still, you know, he was totally mortified.

DD: It is a good thing when patients get funnier.

JW: Absolutely. Maybe that's what I did for him; a kind of greater sweetness and humour. But he was still hiding after four years.

DD: I notice that when students become interested in psychoanalytic diag-nostics, they always diagnose themselves as obsessional. Even a lot of psycho-analysts diagnose themselves as such. It's not a fun diagnosis...

JW: I would never diagnose myself as obsessional, though my obsessional aspects did come to the surface late in my analysis, which was important, especially for having more empathy for this diagnosis and not seeing it merely as the enemy. There would be no space with respect to trauma and jouissance if it wasn't for the obsessional attempt to understand, space, defend, fortify, know. It's just that all the meaning piles on. How do you help someone get out from under the weight of 'understanding'? There is a hesitation to that position, and some moralism and superiority. This is how the jouissance returns. One can wait forever and stay in the 'know'.

DD: I suppose we can only hope to keep encountering our Dora's, so they keep us awake! Thanks a lot for your time!

JW: You're welcome!

Chapter 11

The Dora Effect and the Formation of the Psychoanalyst

The Enigma of Clinical Formation

Starting with the question "Who's your Dora?", we ended up with the "Dora effect!" As Patricia Gherovici explains, the Dora effect refers to those analysands who teach us how to become better analysts. Each interview indicated that the question of Dora – and the multiplication of Dora's – ultimately boiled down to questions of clinical formation. This may not come as a surprise, as I already referenced Freud and Lacan in the introduction and their impact on the elaboration of psychoanalysis through clinical encounters. However, it does indicate that this effect is not merely a historical artifact but is rather essential to the development of psychoanalysis and the clinical development of psychoanalysts.

The question that arises then, is what it means to be "formed" as a psychoanalyst. Clinical formation seems to be constructed against a backdrop of enigmatic factors and mysteries (Kruger, 2002). According to Safouan (1983), psychoanalysts would readily admit three central points about their training: first, it has nothing to do with the reproduction of a model; second, it has nothing to do with the transmission of a know-how; third, no one can practice analysis without having undergone analysis oneself. The interviews in this book illustrate a fourth essential point, which may be harder to admit, and we hardly (publicly) talk about: the contingent encounters with our patients. The enigma of clinical formation is not situated solely on one of these points but concern a desire to be awakened.

Carried by Desire

In clinical practice, patients have the power to surprise and move us. Those who think that clinical work will leave them indifferent will quickly be proven wrong. Every practicing analyst knows that analysis does not necessarily have the tranquil allure of a walk on a mild autumn evening (Silvestre, 1982). Sooner or later, everyone has an encounter with a patient who will shake them up. The interviewees showed how such experiences can be formative, if

DOI: 10.4324/9781003410935-11

this is carried by desire. Without a doubt, we all know there will be no shortage of defeats, which can be paralysing and make us want to flee clinical practice, but it can also put one to work.

What will be provoked by clinical work is one's unconscious, as there is always the risk of using one's own phantasm, neurosis, psychosis, or perversion as a reference for our clinical practice (Cid Vivas, 2002). Consequently, the fundamental principle that structures all our clinical work is one of passionate ignorance: 'I-don't-want-to-know-anything-about-it'.

Each case will push the analyst to their limits, and as a result, they will have no other recourse than their relationship to psychoanalysis, the theoretical and ethical framework in which they have chosen to situate themselves (Skriabine, 2002). This is the position that Freud consistently maintained when constructing psychoanalysis. He continually returned to his elaboration, incorporating clinical experience, relying on what was for him a stumbling block, on what seemed to contradict his previous theoretical construction, on what appeared to have no place in it. He never let go of what was problematic and never succumbed to the desire to know nothing about what was going on. It was a courageous endeavour. This was the main difference between Breuer and Freud and how psychoanalysis started (Geerardyn, 1993). The encounter with Anna O. was an endpoint for Breuer. This made him further reflect on his cases from a strictly medical ethical point of view. For Freud, this case was a starting point. Later, Emmy von N. helped him introduce the psycho-cathartic method and his encounter with Cacillie M. resulted in the *Preliminary Communication* (Freud, 1955 [1893]) and the *Studies on Hysteria* (Freud, 1955 [1893]). To process his encounter with Dora, he kept writing and thinking about what went wrong and, in the end, he was able to pinpoint his mistake.

Freud demonstrated in a paradigmatic way the openness to the effect-of-formation carried by desire. Without a doubt, a desire without formation is blind and a formation without desire is empty (Cottet, 2002, p. 75). The Dora effect concerns the idea that if one has this desire, a modification of the analyst's position in relation to knowledge is possible, and this can change the clinical practice of an analyst.

Of course, one's clinical practice changes because of cumulative experience. Miller (2002b) pointed out that, Freud did not analyse the *Young Homosexual* (Freud, 1955 [1920]) in the same way as he did Dora (1953 [1901]). He learned from the lesson that Dora had given him. Similarly, Lacan's clinic is not the same when he analysed the case of Little Hans in his fourth Seminar (Lacan, 2022 [1956–1957]) as when he took it up again in 1975 at the Geneva Conference on the Symptom. However, it is mostly contingent encounters with patients that play a major role. These encounters can be discussed in supervision and analysis or serve as material for elaborating psychoanalytic theory.

The Dora Effect and the Formation of the Psychoanalyst 117

A Formational Sequence

If clinical formation can only be present if it is carried by desire, it is because this formation has a specific sequence: there is an encounter with a lack-in-knowledge, which creates a subjective division, and this can result in an elaboration of knowledge (Brodsky, 2002).

This encounter does not only concern what we lack in knowledge, but also puts a lack, a hole, in what we think we know all too well. This creates a subjective division. One must be able to bear this. The phantasm (of mastery) is always around the corner, ready to close the gap that the real of absolute contingency opens in clinical practice. Some clinicians prefer to position themselves in the master or university discourse and hold on to knowledge. Many practitioners retreat, returning to the practice of psychotherapy or psychiatry, or other practices of the master's discourse, which allow, better than psychoanalysis, to suture this lack in the Other. Accordingly, analytical training is not so much about accumulating knowledge as it is about going against one's repression (Miller, 2002a).

Consequently, in their formation, the relation to knowledge is paradoxical for the analyst. As Lacan states in his *Variations on the Standard Treatment* (Lacan, 2002, p. 290): "True formation always consists in knowing how to ignore what one knows." The formation of a psychoanalyst begins where formation usually ends, precisely, at completeness (which is often awarded with a degree). It is a desire for a formation in reverse (Mazotti, 2002), a desire for a 'university deformation' (Cottet, 2002). Having this desire will, like for Freud and Lacan, allow one to reach untrodden grounds.

The provocation or encounter with a lack in knowledge will always be a contingent one and as such, this sequence cannot be planned, nor can it be automated. There is no automatism of the analytic formation, only the possibility of making room for contingency (Miller, 2002c).

Compelled to Write

Each case puts the psychoanalyst and psychoanalysis to a radical test, at stake are the psychoanalyst's knowledge and the theory of psychoanalysis. This is why such encounters often compel the analyst to write about them, as there is a certain provocation to an elaboration of knowledge, a certain formalization that confronts the case with psychoanalytic theory. It becomes a back-and-forth between theory and practice.

Lacan (1975 [1953–1954]) insists that psychoanalysis must be reinvented for each person. It is an enlightened practice, and the analyst must be able to give a reasoned account of it. Thus, each analyst must build their own understanding of the experience and its foundations in the particular and on a case-by-case basis, reformulating the theory in their own way and inventing the style that will mark their practice and way of life, integrating elaborated knowledge and their own experience. This involves their relation to the signifier and knowledge, on the one hand, and the way in which they have learned to cope with their mode of jouissance, on the other.

By elaborating on cases, the analyst confronts their knowledge and non-knowledge with 'others, who are also marked by effects-of-formation. This concerns the supervisory practice of psychoanalysis. Listening to other ways of reading, hearing and knowing allows the analyst to see where there was a blind spot, or an obviousness hidden from them. They can rectify misunderstandings, correct their mistakes, and confirm their comprehensions (Skriabine, 2002). It is clear that one cannot do it alone. One needs an analyst, a supervisor, colleagues, a Psychoanalytic School, and Zen-Buddhist Masters.

The Desire of the Analyst

When there is a Dora effect it is because, as we saw with Freud, patients make clear that through our position, there is a closure of the unconscious. The radical act of a psychoanalyst is giving the unconscious of the analysand the opportunity to appear (Miller, 1994). Some patients will make clear to their analyst that they are not positioning themselves correctly. Some will make clear that there is no analyst present for them. With no psychoanalyst present, there is no psychoanalysis.

Lacan highlighted that what is at stake in the analytic training is the desire of the analyst. The desire of the analyst should be a question for the analysand – for example, "What does all of this want to say?" "What's the meaning of all of this?" "All that I'm saying, me, the analysand, what does all of this really want to say" (Miller, 2010, p. 115)? Miller (2010) states we achieve wonderful effects with this, only on the condition that the desire of the analyst stays veiled. It is not easy for the analyst to be in the correct position (Naveau, 2003). The analyst – this is a rule, Freud says – must never give anything to the analysand that comes from his own unconscious. In each case, he must detach himself from his countertransference (Miller, 2002b). Working with Dora, Freud was not positioning himself in the analytic discourse, but in the master's discourse. His desire was not veiled. He got duped by his countertransference. Countertransference exactly consists in the analyst coming out of his objective position to support his own subjective position (Stevens, in Miller 2002). When an analyst believes they are a master, think they are the clever one, when they dress their act in narcissism, when they like their patients a bit too much, when they think they understand, when they orient themselves through their own unconscious, they surpass their act (Laurent, 2002). These analysands first of all become our Dora's exactly because they pinpoint the lapses in our psychoanalytic act and second, because the analyst has the desire to acknowledge the surpassing of their act and takes it up in supervision or analysis. Supervision is about "supervising a subject that surpasses his act" (Lacan, 2001 [1967]). This indicates that the effect-of-formation is integral to the analytic act (Monribot, 2002). The moment where one starts to consult a supervisor is mostly because a patient has made clear one is not positioned in the analytic discourse (Dulsster, 2022). Supervision makes it possible to question the position of the analyst overwhelmed or exceeded by their act, and to refocus the orientation of the treatment (Laurent, 2002).

Formation of the Unconscious

If our Dora's pinpoint where we have surpassed our analytic act, it is because every direction of the treatment is always conditioned by the point of consequence an analyst has arrived at in their own analysis (Lacan, 2002 [1957]). Freud as well, in his 'Future Prospects of Psychoanalysis' (1910), indicated that no psychoanalyst goes further than permitted by his own complexes and internal resistances. He stated that we should consequently require that analysts begin the activity of the analytic practice with a self-analysis and continually carry it deeper while they are making their observations on their patients. He even goes so far as to say that anyone who fails to produce results in a self-analysis of this kind may at once give up any idea of being able to treat patients by analysis.

Not every patient has the same effect, not every patient can become a 'Dora', not every remark will resonate. After the interview with Annie Rogers, I asked her if there was one question that she would like to ask to the other interviewees. Her reply was a question that slumbers in every interview: "How is everyone's Dora case connected to their unconscious?" Indeed, the unconscious signs it letters.

What is at stake in one's own analysis is the formation of the unconscious. Lacan (1973) stated as well that there is no formation of the analyst, only formation of the unconscious. Consequently, Lacan puts the personal analysis at the centre of the formation of the analyst. In Vincennes (Lacan, 2001 [1975]) he states, "that the analyst must take support of what he holds from his own analysis". As such, one is only assumed to be operating as an analyst because she has been made capable of doing so (Miller, 2002c).

Consequently, it could be said that Lacan did not hold much regard for the formative effects of clinical work. Miller even stated that he mocks it, as he sees in it a certain routine, a deadening, a forgetting of what is at stake (Miller, 2002c). However, one cannot ignore the fact that there is a certain tension and interaction between one's own analysis and one's clinical practice. The fact that a practicing psychoanalyst remains in analysis while conducting treatments has the effect that their practice itself is a part of their analysis. Consequently, practicing analysts can treat in their analysis, as an integral part of it, the subjective problems that their own practice may cause them. If there is 'an analyst', there is a desire to be put to work or take up the work their clinical practice brought them, this prevents their clinical practice from becoming deadening. The analysing analyst will be able to work on dissecting their position and be given the opportunity to work through these subjective issues.

What every interview made clear, it's that a clinician can be awakened if their desire allows it.

Having come to this conclusion. Only one question remains to be asked: "Who's your Dora?"

References

Brodsky, G. (2002). Effet d'un contrôle. Clinique de la formation dans la psychanalyse. *Quarto*, 76, 78–79.

Cid Vivas, H. (2002). La croix de l'analyste. *La Cause du Désir*, 52, 57–59.

Cottet, S. (2002). Autonomie du contrôle. *La Cause du Désir*, 52, 75–77.

Dulsster, D. (2022). *The Reign of Speech*. Palgrave, Basingstoke.

Freud, S. (1955 [1893]). Studies on Hysteria. *Standard Edition*, II, 1–312.

Freud, S. (1955 [1893]). On the Psychical Mechanism of Hysterical Phenomena: Preliminary Communication. In Freud (1955 [1893]). Studies on Hysteria. *Standard Edition*, II, 1–18.

Freud, S. (1910). The Future Prospects of Psychoanalytic Therapy. *Standard Edition*, XI, 139–152. The Hogarth Press, London.

Freud, S. (1953 [1901]). Fragments of an Analysis of a Case of Hysteria. *Standard Edition*, VII, 1–122. The Hogarth Press, London.

Freud, S. (1955 [1920]). The Psychogenesis of a Case of Homosexuality in a Woman. *Standard Edition*, XVIII, 145–174. The Hogarth Press, London.

Geerardyn, F. (1993). *Freuds Psychologie van het Oordeel*. Idesça, Gent.

Kruger, F. (2002). Les défauts d'une formation. *La Cause du Désir*, 52, 61–63.

Lacan, J. (2022 [1956–1957]). *The Seminar Book IV: The Object Relation*. Polity Press, Oxford.

Lacan, J. (2001 [1967]). Discourse à l'Ecole Freudienne de Paris. *Autres Ecrits* (pp. 261–281). Seuil, Paris.

Lacan, J. (2001 [1975]). Peut-être à Vincennes. *Autres Ecrits* (pp. 313–315). Seuil, Paris.

Lacan, J. (2002 [1955]). Variations on the Standard Treatment. In *Ecrits* (pp. 197–268) [English ed. translated by Bruce Fink]. Norton.

Lacan, J. (2002 [1957]). Direction of the Treatment and the Principles of its Power. In *Ecrits* (pp. 489–542) [English ed. Translated by Bruce Fink]. Norton.

Lacan, J. (1973). *Intervention at IEFP on 3 Novembre 1973*, Lettres de l'EFP, 15.

Lacan, J. (1975 [1953–1954]). *Le Séminaire: Les écrits techniques de Freud*. Seuil, Paris.

Laurent, E., Stevens, A., Tarrab, M., and Torres, M. (2002). Entretien sur la formation. *La Cause du Désir*, 52, 95–98.

Mazotti, M. (2002). Une formation infinie? *La Cause du Désir*, 52, 55–57.

Miller, J.-A. (1994). Le cartel dans le Monde. Intervention à la Journée des Cartels du 8 octobre 1994 à L'ECF. Available at: https://www.causefreudienne.net/cartelscartels-dans-les-textes/.

Miller, J.-A. (2002a). Le débat. *La Cause du Désir*, 52, 77–85.

Miller, J.-A. (2002b). *Cours du 6 février: Réflexions sur le moment présent 4* [*Lesson of the 6th of February: Reflections on the Present Time, 4*], Orientation Lacanianne III (Unpublished).

Miller, J.-A. (2002c). Pour introduire l'effet-de-formation. *Quarto*, 76, 4–7.

Miller, J.-A. (2010). Passe du Parlêtre. *La Cause du Désir*, 74, 113–123.

Monribot, P. (2002). Formation et satisfaction. *La Cause du Désir*, 52, 59–61.

Naveau, P. (2003). La Psychanalyse Appliquée au Symptôme: Enjeux et Problèmes. *Pertinences de la Psychanalyse Appliquée*. Seuil, Paris. 15–23.

Safouan, M. (1983). *Jacques Lacan et la Question de la Formation des Analystes*. Éditions du Seuil, Paris.

Silvestre, M. (1982). Rapport introductif. Dix-sept Exposés sur les Moments Cruciaux dans la Cure Analytique. *Cause Freudienne*, 3, 6–8.

Skriabine, P. (2002). Effets de vérité, effet-de-formation, savoir du psychanalyste. Treize aperçus sur la question. *La Cause du Désir*, 52, 50–54.

Stevens, A. (2002). Le débat. In J.-A. Miller, *La Cause du Désir*, 52, 77–85.

Index

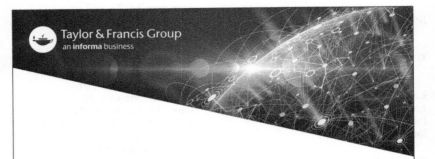

For Product Safety Concerns and Information please contact our EU
representative GPSR@taylorandfrancis.com Taylor & Francis Verlag GmbH,
Kaufingerstraße 24, 80331 München, Germany

Printed and bound by CPI Group (UK) Ltd, Croydon, CR0 4YY
08/06/2025
01897002-0016